What Are You Doing After the Dance?

How to Continue Celebrating Once the Celebration is Over

25TH ANNIVERSARY REVISED EDITION

SHANE WALL

Godly Writes PUBLISHING

Godly Writes Publishing, LLC
Orangeburg, SC

Copyright © 2025 by Shane Wall

All rights reserved. No part of this publication may be reproduced, stored in a retrieval system, or transmitted in any form or by any means, electronic, mechanical, recording or otherwise, without the prior, written permission of the publisher.

Published by:
Godly Writes Publishing
P. O. Box 2005
Orangeburg SC 29116-2005

Unless otherwise noted, Scripture quotations taken from the Amplified® Bible (AMPC),

Copyright © 1954, 1958, 1962, 1964, 1965, 1987 by The Lockman Foundation

Used by permission. lockman.org

Scripture quotations marked KJV are taken from the King James Version of the Bible.

Public Domain.

What Are You Doing After the Dance?: 25th Anniversary Revised Edition

ISBN: 978-0-9967997-7-5

Disclaimers:

This book is a work of nonfiction. The stories and testimonies shared are accurate to the best of the author's knowledge and are presented to bring biblical insight and understanding. The content of this book is not intended to replace professional advice for spiritual, emotional, or psychological issues.

The name satan and related terms are intentionally not capitalized in this book, except when appearing in direct Scripture quotations or beginning a sentence. This decision reflects our choice to deny him the dignity of recognition, even at the expense of conventional grammar.

10 9 8 7 6 5 4 3 2 1

For Worldwide Distribution, Printed in the U.S.A.

WWW.SHANEWALL.COM

DEDICATION

Over the past 25 years, two of the brightest lights in my life have been you, Joshua and Amayah. I pray and desire to be the best father to you, both naturally and spiritually. I love you deeply and look forward to witnessing every one of your lives' dances and the God-ordained moments that follow. Be blessed always. I love you more than words can ever say.

-Daddy

TABLE OF CONTENTS

Introduction 7
Chapter 1: **The Dance (A Scenario)** 11
Chapter 2: **After the Love Dance** 21
Chapter 3: **May I Have This Dance?** 27
Chapter 4: **After the Friend Dance** 31
Chapter 5: **After the Graduation Dance** 37
Chapter 6: **Decision Brings Destiny to the Dance** 41
Chapter 7: **After the Society Dance** 55
Chapter 8: **When Loneliness Keeps You Company** 63
Chapter 9: **After the Society Dance** 69
Chapter 10: **Are You Ignorant?** 73
Chapter 11: **Glory After the Dance** 83
Chapter 12: **The Beauty of an Opened Grave** 93
Altar Call and Prayer for Salvation 101
About the Author 103
Contact 104

INTRODUCTION

In 1986, the year I graduated from Orangeburg-Wilkinson High School, I envisioned writing a book. Fourteen years later, the vision is reality. I have drawn on my experience as an evangelist, a business manager, and a devoted believer of God's Word during the past year to write it. Late nights and early mornings often found me studying scriptures for appropriate documentation. It is only natural that I learned more of the gospel from the Bible. I used this knowledge as commandments and guidelines for the reader to follow in pursuing a life that is pleasing in the sight of God.

In no way could I have conveyed my purpose without my spiritual and religious conviction. It is my sincere prayer that every reader, while reading this book, will understand how to continue celebrating the life that God gave them even after each celebration. I also pray that you will feel the joy, partake of the Word, and know the answer to: What are you doing after the dance?

(The above was originally published in 2000)

Wow. When I reread the introduction I wrote twenty-five years ago, I felt a connection to my younger self, a much younger man who was deeply hungry for God's Word and passionate about blessing others through it. That same hunger still fuels me today, driving me to pray and read daily, fast each week, and teach whenever the opportunity arises.

I first preached the message "What Are You Doing After the Dance?" in my twenties, at Faith Tabernacle Deliverance Temple in Orangeburg, South Carolina. For more than a year after that sermon, people in the congregation continued referring to it. Many urged me to turn the message into a book. The Holy Spirit confirmed it: I was supposed to do just that.

That same year, my mom bought me a personal computer on Black Friday from Walmart. It was on that computer that I taught myself to type without looking at the keyboard, knowing I'd need to memorize the keys if I was going to write an entire book.

Even so, I often stalled. I kept praying for the money to publish the book until the Holy Spirit asked me, "Why are you praying for money when you haven't finished writing it?" I realized then that provision would come after obedience, so I refocused and completed the manuscript.

I sent the finished book to several publishers, and all of them turned me down—except for one who wanted $10,000. I didn't have anything close to that amount.

That's when I discovered self-publishing. I bought a book on Christian self-publishing and learned the process. The money came just as God said it would. One key resource He used was my sister, Rhette. She asked what I wanted for my birthday, and I jokingly told her the exact dollar amount I needed to take the next major step in publishing the book. She mailed a birthday card to me with a check for that precise amount and a note that read, "Be careful what you ask for because you might get it."

Her generosity touched me deeply, and with that, I published "What Are You Doing After the Dance?" in December 2000.

As you read this 25th Anniversary Revised Edition, note that the tone of this book differs from that of my more recent works. That's intentional. "What Are You Doing After the Dance?" was my very first book, written in my twenties, with the voice, passion, and perspective I had at the time. Although the content has been carefully edited, I chose to preserve much of the original style and approach, primarily since this book addresses a younger audience—those in their teens and twenties who are navigating identity, purpose, and God's plan for their lives.

While adults will certainly enjoy and be impacted by this message, this book may not reflect the same level of writing found in my later works. Still, what it may lack in maturity of style, it makes up for in sincerity, clarity, revelation, and a deep desire to share the truth of God's love and calling.

I pray that you'll feel the heart behind every page, and that this 25th Anniversary Revised Edition blesses you just as powerfully now as it did for many people a generation ago. Thank you for embracing the message in this book and allowing it to take root in your heart. I love you with the love of the Lord, and I'm so grateful for the pleasure of planting these words in your hearts.

Be blessed!
Shane Wall

CHAPTER 1:

THE DANCE (A SCENARIO)

> *12 And it was told King David, The Lord has blessed the house of Obed-edom and all that belongs to him because of the ark of God. So David went and brought up the ark of God from the house of Obed-edom into the City of David with rejoicing;*
> *13 And when those who bore the ark of the Lord had gone six paces, he sacrificed an ox and a fatling.*
> *14 And David danced before the Lord with all his might, clad in a linen ephod [a priest's upper garment].*
> *15 So David and all the house of Israel brought up the ark of the Lord with shouting and with the sound of the trumpet.*
> *16 As the ark of the Lord came into the City of David, Michal, Saul's daughter [David's wife], looked out of the window and saw King David leaping and dancing before the Lord, and she despised him in her heart.*
>
> 2 Samuel 6:12–16 AMPC

A dance is a celebration.

A man spots a woman standing alone at a party. He approaches and asks, "Would you like to dance?" She agrees. They spend time dancing, laughing, and getting to know each other gradually. As the night unfolds, the man finally works up the courage to ask the question that's been burning in his heart: "What are you doing after the dance?"

Now the woman is faced with a decision. She realizes his question could be about more than simply grabbing coffee; it could suggest intimacy. She weighs her answer carefully, knowing it will either open a door or firmly close it.

God's Invitation After Your Celebration

Before we continue the story, let's bring this into your spiritual life.

God has blessed you mightily: He's healed your body, delivered you from an addiction, sent you a breakthrough, or answered a long-awaited prayer. Your heart bursts with praise. You sing, you dance, and you shout hallelujah!

Then, while you're still basking in that joy, the Holy Spirit taps you on the shoulder and gently asks, "What are you doing after the dance?"

Going back to the scenario, the woman could respond, "I don't know."

Think about that spiritually. You're in a powerful service. The Word of God is going forth. Miracles are happening. People are being set free. The presence of God is thick in the atmosphere. You dance with joy, swept away by His goodness.

Then the Holy Spirit asks you, "What are you doing after the dance?"

And your answer is "I don't know."

After all God has done—after He poured His Word and power into your life—you still don't know what your next step will be?

A moment of celebration means nothing if it isn't followed by commitment.

Another response you or I could give is "I'm going home." God delivered and revived me. I've just received a financial breakthrough. My child just gave their heart to the Lord, but I'm going back to the same old place I just came from: home. I've decided not to go any further. I've just been set free, and I'm going home.

Home is a comfortable place. At home, you don't have to strive for growth. You're back in your old environment, surrounded by familiar habits. At home, you don't have to care how you look spiritually. It's the place where you let your guard down, fall back into routine, and simply exist.

Are you the one giving this response to God? After all He's done, are you just going home? Going back to the same mindset, the same habits, the same weak prayers, and the same easy compromises? Yes, you've danced, you've celebrated—but you've decided to return to your comfort zone. Does this look like you?

Again, let's return to the scenario. The third possible response to "What are you doing after the dance?" implies a sense of intimacy. It's an answer that accepts a perceived invitation to closeness if the lady says to the gentleman, "Whatever you want me to do."

You can almost feel the excitement rising between them. Their connection builds. They want to leave the party. Their space has suddenly become too crowded. They're not interested in the noise; they want each other. They want closeness, quiet, and connection. Why? Because they both desire the same thing, and they've been honest about it.

Then they leave the dance and go to a place of seclusion.

Spiritually, "Whatever You want me to do…" is the response God desires most. It's our way of saying to God: "You've captured my heart, and I want to be with You forever."

Jesus' Response After the Dance

Jesus healed the sick, raised the dead, multiplied food, and cast out demons. All of that was worthy of celebration. But what did Jesus do after the dance? What was His response to the Father's will?

> *Saying, Father, if You are willing, remove this cup from Me; yet not My will, but [always] Yours be done.*
>
> Luke 22:42 AMPC

Even though Jesus wished the cup of suffering could pass, He chose to submit to it. He pleased the Father by obeying—even when it was painful. Jesus is our example. We please God by submitting our will to His. It's what we do after the dance that shows where our hearts truly lie.

As saints, we have a secret place where only God's presence resides. In that place, loneliness disappears. Worry and sorrow dissolve. Disappointment loses its power. Joy lives there—*absolute* joy, which is different from happiness. Joy is a response through the Holy Spirit (Galatians 5:22). Happiness is based on the emotional feelings of perceived "good luck" or "pleasurable circumstances."

Joy isn't natural; it's supernatural. It doesn't depend on emotion but on spiritual truth. Joy is how the Spirit responds to anxiety, sorrow, and disappointment.

Sorrow and Joy Together

When my uncle, George Thompson, a pastor, passed away, I felt both sorrow and joy. I grieved his absence but rejoiced knowing he was with the Lord. My sorrow came from emotion, and my joy came from the Spirit.

This type of reaction to adverse circumstances is what it means to walk in the Spirit—responding to every situation with fruit, not flesh.

> *22 But the fruit of the [Holy] Spirit [the work which His presence within accomplishes] is love, joy (gladness), peace, patience (an even temper, forbearance), kindness, goodness (benevolence), faithfulness,*
> *23 Gentleness (meekness, humility), self-control (self-restraint, continence). Against such things there is no law [that can bring a charge].*
>
> Galatians 5:22–23 AMPC

> *For the rest, brethren, whatever is true, whatever is worthy of reverence and is honorable and seemly, whatever is just, whatever is pure, whatever is lovely and lovable, whatever is kind and winsome and gracious, if there is any virtue and excellence, if there is anything worthy of praise, think on and weigh and take account of these things [fix your minds on them].*
>
> Philippians 4:8 AMPC

These virtues are more than behaviors; they're locations where our minds should dwell. To live this way is to live in the Spirit. That's how we walk with Him.

The Heart of Intimacy

Intimacy with God produces these virtues and can cause us to forget the dance because we've become consumed with Him.

The word "intimacy" means to reveal what's deepest within with no formality. God desires that with you. He wants the real you, not your church clothes or your ministry title.

There have been times after I ministered when people didn't know the fire still burning inside of me. I'd sit in my car, worshiping God, still feeling His presence. I'd pour out my heart to Him, and He would touch me again in such a powerful way I couldn't even explain it.

That's an *after the dance* experience—one worth continuing.

Confess to God After the Dance

Confess means to be truthful with God. Say to Him, "Lord, I don't want anyone else to see this, but I need You to. Something has me bound, and I want to be free." God sees everything, but He only touches what we expose to Him. This kind of spiritual nakedness declares, "I meant it when I said, 'Whatever You want me to do.'"

The enemy hides in the darkness. God works in the light. When we give Him full access, He'll work in us through the intimate moments we enjoy in private with Him.

I live every day confronting the parts of me that still need God's touch. Whether I'm driving, walking, or waiting for food, I repent. I live a lifestyle of repentance because I know I could become a casualty on Judgment Day if I don't. I don't want to be one of the people who worked for Jesus but never truly knew Him (Matthew 7:22-23). So I bring every part of Shane before the Lord. Jesus made forgiveness possible through His blood. I want to be ready when He comes!

From Presents to Presence

You've enjoyed the dance. But now the dance is over. Are you willing to enjoy *God's* company? You might ask, "Is exposing myself to God an enjoyment?" Yes. To be that close to Him is joy beyond words.

> *Come close to God and He will come close to you...*
>
> James 4:8 AMPC

When God draws near, deliverance comes. But if nothing is exposed, nothing can be delivered. Deliverance is joy. Deliverance is freedom. And freedom comes to those who cry out to God.

> 1 I waited patiently and expectantly for the Lord; and He inclined to me and heard my cry.
> 2 He drew me up out of a horrible pit [a pit of tumult and of destruction], out of the miry clay (froth and slime), and set my feet upon a rock, steadying my steps and establishing my goings.
>
> Psalm 40:1–2 AMPC

The Offerings (Intimacy)

> 17 They brought in the ark of the Lord and set it in its place inside the tent which David had pitched for it, and David offered burnt offerings and peace offerings before the Lord.
> 18 When David had finished offering the burnt offerings and the peace offerings, he blessed the people in the name [and presence] of the Lord of hosts.
>
> 2 Samuel 6:17–18 AMPC

The burnt offering that David offered before the Lord was a voluntary offering. The burnt offering was the only offering that the offerer had to burn until the fire consumed it entirely. The burning itself had to be gradual to ensure it lasted from morning to evening. Another acceptable custom was that the burning had to last from one daily sacrifice to the next. The command was that during the sacrifice, the fire should never be allowed to go out.

Peace offerings were expressions of thanksgiving, vows, or freewill devotion. The offerer conducting the sacrifice sprinkled blood, burned the fat, and shared the remaining meat among the participants. He then lifted the breast and shoulder and waved them before God as a sign of reverence. The family enjoyed the rest of the meat. (Leviticus 7:19–21)

David completed the full offering—nothing halfhearted. Scripture says he *"had made an end"* of the offerings, which means he kept going until he finished the job. Not rushing or leaving early is the kind of intimacy God wants. Afterward, David blessed the people by sharing bread, meat, and drink with them. He didn't leave them empty.

Michal's Response

> 19 And distributed among all the people, the whole multitude of Israel, both to men and women, to each a cake of bread, a portion of meat, and a cake of raisins. So all the people departed, each to his house.
>
> 20 Then David returned to bless his household. And [his wife] Michal daughter of Saul came out to meet David and said, How glorious was the king of Israel today, who stripped himself of his kingly robes and uncovered himself in the eyes of his servants' maids as one of the worthless fellows shamelessly uncovers himself!
>
> 2 Samuel 6:19–20 AMPC

David went home ready to bless his family, but Michal confronted him with sarcasm and shame. She may have still been angry after being taken from her second husband, or maybe she simply misunderstood David's intimacy with God.

What matters is that her response shows what *she* did after the dance. The dance isn't always physical; it includes every experience where God touches your life. If someone doesn't know your story, they may not understand your praise.

So what do *you* do after someone else's dance? Will you rejoice with them or criticize them? We'll deal with that more in a later chapter.

After the Dance: Keep Moving Forward

David spent a long time offering before the Lord. He did all of this and more after the dance.

Maybe you're still waiting for your dance moment—your breakthrough, your healing, or your miracle. Perhaps it's been a while since you've danced.

The truth is, many people plan what they're going to do after the dance before they even arrive at the celebration. Plan your intimacy with God now!

A preacher once said, "Don't wait till the battle is over. Dance now!"

By faith, you can dance now! Without faith, it's impossible to please God. Dance in faith, knowing that God has already declared you victorious.

So go ahead—dance now! Just make sure you already know what you're going to do *after* the dance.

As I write this book, I don't yet know everything God plans to do through it. But when it's published, I know I'm going to dance! Still, that dance won't be the end of my exertion. Even now, before the dance happens, I'm already seeking and listening to God, asking what He wants me to do after the celebration.

We always want God to do things for us. After He blesses us, what are we supposed to do for Him? The answer is simple: Replace lip service with labor.

> *Therefore, my beloved brethren, be firm (steadfast), immovable, always abounding in the work of the Lord [always being superior, excelling, doing more than enough in the service of the Lord], knowing and being continually aware that your labor in the Lord is not futile [it is never wasted or to no purpose].*
>
> 1 Corinthians 15:58 AMPC

In this verse of the Bible, the Greek word for "always" means "every when." We're called to abound in the work of the Lord at all times: When we feel like it. When we don't. When people understand why we're tired. When we're discouraged, disappointed, or drained. No matter which "when" comes, God can still find us abounding in His work.

In the original Greek, the word *labor* isn't just about the effort; it's about the *weariness* that follows the effort.

Jesus expects our labor to lead to weariness. But He doesn't respond by demanding more. Instead, He sees our weariness and calls it good. Then, He shares that our labor is never in vain. Jesus doesn't leave His workers physically drained without offering relief. He calls us to Himself for rest.

CHAPTER 1: THE DANCE (A SCENARIO)

Come to Me, all you who labor and are heavy-laden and overburdened, and I will cause you to rest. [I will ease and relieve and refresh your souls.]

Matthew 11:28 AMPC

Rest isn't about quitting. It's about being refreshed and strengthened for the next assignment. Jesus gives you rest, not to pause your purpose, but to support and empower you to continue.

Support in the Kingdom of God here on Earth doesn't happen automatically. It must be built intentionally. We are required to carry our end of the load. Many don't recognize the urgency of the hour, as in a distracted surgeon engaging in cruel joking while performing a critical surgery. But time is calling for your fruit. If you're not producing, you're out of season. You may have started slow, but don't stop! God is still requiring a harvest from you.

Not everyone immediately rises into their purpose because it requires effort—mental, physical, spiritual, and emotional. We must first realize that we do have a purpose. God will reveal it to us if we ask. He's ready to train us, lead us, and prepare us.

Being saved and filled with the Holy Spirit is just the beginning. Kingdom life calls for labor. As we walk with the Holy Spirit, He will lead us to every person, every place, and every opportunity necessary to fulfill our callings.

I used to think I had changed direction too many times in life. Now I realize every shift served my purpose. Every school experience, every job, every painful or difficult choice—they all shaped me. Today, I use the wisdom and knowledge those seasons gave me, and I am more fulfilled now than ever before.

Purpose turns everything you've lived through into preparation for where God is taking you. God sees you. His eye is on the sparrow, and it is certainly on you.

I consider myself one of God's little ones. Yet, God is using me, and He will use you also.

Let's not leave God or our purpose… after the dance.

CHAPTER 2:

AFTER THE LOVE DANCE

The term 'love dance' refers to the moment when someone finds true love.

"How do you know when you love somebody?" I've asked that question many times. Most people respond the same way: "I can feel it. That's how I know I love him or her." I take issue with that answer. I don't believe a feeling should identify love. Some may disagree with me, but hear this: Love is not a feeling, because even when the feeling goes, we still have to love. If love were only a feeling, it would be unstable and unreliable. And true love isn't like that. Love doesn't vanish just because emotion does. Love remains.

There have been countless examples of divorced couples who still feel a deep connection. Even after a painful or "messy" divorce, they may find themselves caring deeply for one another, whether they say it out loud or not. They love each other, perhaps quietly but undeniably.

It's my prayer that you genuinely understand what I'm trying to convey. Once you stop identifying love as a fleeting emotion, you'll begin to see who you truly love—and who truly loves you.

What does it mean to find love? Usually, it refers to the moment someone begins to experience genuine, lasting love. If you believe you've found true love, then you've had your *love dance*. But the question is, what happens after the dance?

True love does not operate on emotions. That may sound strange, but agape love—the love of God—isn't based on emotion. It's the love we are called to show everyone. Love is a fruit of the Spirit, not a product of feelings. If the only love you know is emotional, then when those emotions fade, so will the love. True love, though, is consistent. It doesn't fluctuate. It looks beyond the faults and recognizes the needs.

Faults vs. Needs

There's a beautiful gospel song that says, "He looked beyond all my faults and saw my needs." For a long time, I thought that meant God looks past our sin and still provides food, clothing, and shelter. But the Lord showed me something deeper: He looks beyond the fault because the need is what causes the fault.

I once asked someone why they smoked. They said, "To calm my bad nerves." I followed up, "If God healed your nerves, would you still need to smoke?" They paused, thought for a moment, and said, "I've never thought about it that way." You see, the fault, smoking, was their response to a more profound need: inner healing. Smoking didn't fix the nerves; it just temporarily dulled the symptoms.

God wants to heal your need so the faults no longer have power over your life. In my book, *Proof: Everyone's Under a Spell*, I share that the stories we believe, the narratives we embrace, and the tales we endorse become spells cast on our lives. Many of the unnecessary faults plaguing our lives today are the result of spells we've accepted and continue to nurture. Freedom is God's plan, not the bondage that spells and curses inflict on our lives.

When you look at people's lives, what do you focus on, their faults or their needs? After your love dance, are you willing to look past the faults of others and recognize their needs? That's what true love does. It sees with compassion. The gospel group, Commissioned, sang it best: "Love isn't love till you've given it away."

You say you've found love, but are you giving it or just receiving it? Many experience love from others but don't extend it in return. If you've had a love dance, you owe it to others to give that love freely.

So, how do you know if you're loved? Some say, "I know it when someone says, 'I love you.'" Others feel loved when they're embraced or when someone goes out of their way to do something for them. But here's the question: What are you doing to show your love? Have you found love, or are you just standing in its glow?

Earlier, I wrote, "Time is calling for your fruit." Love is a fruit of the Spirit, and when love is alive, it produces more fruit: joy, peace, longsuffering, kindness, goodness, faithfulness, gentleness, and self-control (Galatians 5:22-23). Love is never out of season. Ecclesiastes 3:8 says there is a time to love and a time to hate. We're called to hate evil, yes, but never to hate people. Love one another, not with fleeting emotions, but with action.

Do you love God? If so, how did you show Him today? Someone once told me, "I prayed and thanked God for what He's done for me." That's good, but gratitude isn't the same as love. Saying, "Thank You…" doesn't prove love. It's a response to generosity, not necessarily evidence of love. So, again, I ask: What did you do today to demonstrate your love for God?

Love always shows. What has your love shown? After you say you love God, where's the evidence? God proved His love by giving. He gave His only begotten Son. That's love. What are you offering in return?

True love gives sacrificially. When you give, are you giving what costs you something or just what you can spare? Real giving doesn't come from your junk drawer; it comes from your heart. You can give without love, but you can't love without giving. People who give only to be seen are not acting from love. Whenever someone asks me for something, I want to give what I'd like to receive, whether it's a gift or my time. That's what love does.

What do you think?

Motive is the heart of action, and not every motive is pure. Purity starts in the mind. God's Word teaches us not just to accept every thought that comes to mind.

> *Finally, brethren, whatsoever things are true, whatsoever things are honest, whatsoever things are just, whatsoever things are pure, whatsoever things are lovely, whatsoever things are of good report; if there be any virtue, and if there be any praise, think on these things.*
>
> Philippians 4:8 KJV

We're supposed to interview each thought first, before we let it go to work within our thinking. How can we interview thoughts? Philippians 4:8 tells us to filter every thought: Is it true? Is it honest? Is it just? Pure? Lovely? Virtuous?

Praiseworthy? If it doesn't pass that test, approved by each of the virtues, we shouldn't even allow it to become a working thought in our minds. Just because something comes to mind doesn't mean it should be hired as a thought.

Have you ever noticed that we think in pictures? If I told you there were three thousand people at church last night, you wouldn't picture the words; you'd see the crowd in your mind. That's why thoughts are so vivid—and why the enemy uses them to tempt us. He plays mental "little movies" of past sins we enjoyed, trying to trap us. But those thoughts aren't always your thoughts. You don't have to own them.

I'll be transparent: There were sins I committed that I enjoyed. The flesh loves sin. Even if you're spiritual, you still live in a fleshly body. Sin wouldn't be tempting if it weren't enjoyable.

> *Choosing rather to suffer affliction with the people of God, than to enjoy the pleasures of sin for a season.*
>
> Hebrews 11:25 KJV

We want to show God how much we love Him by obeying His Word. Obedience can become difficult because we're constantly facing temptations that demons tailor perfectly to satisfy our selfish desires.

Here's something that works: When a demon plays a "little movie" in your mind, showing you how pleasurable giving in to a temptation will feel, finish the movie with reality, not just the fun part. We must take responsibility to complete the ending scene of the mental movie ourselves because demons never show the guilt, the shame, and the devastating consequences that follow the act. When we add the ending, we'll show ourselves the discouraging confrontation, the unwanted regret, and the ill-gotten broken trust, all resulting from one or more acts of sinful pleasure.

That ending often keeps me from stepping back into sin. Thoughts affect us because we allow them to. We hired them. And what we hire will always start working immediately. What is worry, after all, but a thought that won't stop working?

> *There is no fear in love [dread does not exist], but full-grown (complete, perfect) love turns fear out of doors and expels every trace of terror! For fear brings with it the thought of punishment, and [so] he who is afraid has not reached the full maturity of love [is not yet grown into love's complete perfection].*
>
> 1 John 4:18 AMPC

Fear causes us to believe the convincing thoughts that something bad will happen. Faith causes us to believe the convincing thoughts that something good will happen. Both are belief systems. Which one are we most likely to entertain first? Which one are we more likely to engage with? To fear the threats of a demon or to have faith in God's promises is a choice we consciously make.

Consider all the people we claim to love. How do we know that we love them? What do we do to prove our love? A tube of toothpaste is decorated on the outside to reflect what's inside. We expect to see the product listed on the label emerge from the tube because we applied pressure to it. When we decorate our lives by labeling ourselves as followers of Jesus Christ, when events in life pressure us, does love for others emerge from our hearts through our actions and words?

Whatever is in us will come out of us, yet some of us find ourselves often deceitful with our words, speaking words of love and care that are not in our hearts. Then, when the time comes to act on our promises, we fail to follow through because we never intended to help, only to sound righteous.

> 6 *Eat not the bread of him who has a hard, grudging, and envious eye, neither desire his dainty foods;*
> 7 *For as he thinks in his heart, so is he. As one who reckons, he says to you, eat and drink, yet his heart is not with you [but is grudging the cost].*
>
> Proverbs 23:6-7 AMPC

God proves His love by giving from His heart. We should do the same. He shared Jesus with the whole world—past, present, and future generations. What are we giving to demonstrate our love for Him?

If you've danced the love dance, then show your love for God and people. Let the evidence of your love be seen in action, sacrifice, obedience, and grace. Now that you've had your love dance…what are you doing after the dance?

CHAPTER 3:

MAY I HAVE THIS DANCE?

"May I have this dance?" is the question asked by someone wanting to dance with another. Are we willing to celebrate another person's victory, even if their win meant our loss? Love is always willing. If someone invites you to dance—to rejoice with them—it's likely they want you there because you matter to them. Scripture teaches, *"Rejoice with those who rejoice…"* (Romans 12:15 AMPC). It's not our job to judge whether someone's moment of celebration is worthy. Just be glad for them. Our time is coming too—and when it does, we'll want someone to dance with us.

Around the age of seven, I became fascinated with gospel radio announcers. My family and I faithfully tuned in to radio station WPJS—*We Proclaim Jesus Saves*. Susan and Cleve were my favorite radio announcers. I often phoned in to answer biblical questions for their "Christian Question" contest, and I won several times. One month, I won so frequently that they told me that I could only win three times per month. I visited the station once to collect my prizes and watched them live on the air. I was starstruck. I always spoke admirably about the announcers. Years later, I became a gospel radio announcer, and to this day, people still compliment my work on the airwaves. God had something in motion even back then. Let's always strive to compliment others, not to receive the same, but to "dance" with them because of what they do so well.

Many people experience great success, but not all can maintain it. Why? A primary reason is the absence of encouragement after the applause fades. During the celebration, encouragement flows freely—but afterward, the celebrant often finds themselves alone. That isolation can be painful and even draining, depleting the necessary motivation to go higher or harder in their efforts.

A friend of mine was a gifted football player. When he excelled in his games, people constantly praised him. But after a serious injury, the cheers dwindled. That sudden silence hurts. The public eye is open to what evokes excitement and awe. Once someone ceases to amaze us, we find no need to celebrate them.

We all need at least one person in our lives who will encourage us no matter what we do or don't do. God, of course, is always there, and if we're honest, we'd like someone in the natural to be physically present with us periodically.

The Holy Spirit is called the Comforter for a reason *(John 16:7)*. God hasn't moved away from you. He's still waiting for you to come closer. And when you do, He'll show you His love, personally, and often through others.

Everyone needs somebody, and everybody wants to be loved by somebody. Will you be that someone for somebody else? Maybe you're thinking, "I would, but I need someone to be there for me first." Let's not forget this principle: "Give, and [gifts] will be given to you..." (Luke 6:38 AMPC). That's not just a feel-good phrase; it's a spiritual law. Whatever you sow into someone else's life will come back into your own in the same or different form, according to God's will for supplying your need. Invest kindness, encouragement, and joy in someone else, and watch it return to you multiplied.

Why be a blessing to someone, even someone who mistreats you? "Bless those who persecute you [who are cruel in their attitude toward you]; bless and do not curse them" (Romans 12:14 AMPC). Doing good deeds for offenders is not easy, but it's indeed powerful and impactful. The individual who mistreats you today may be the vessel God uses to bless you tomorrow.

I remember dining at a nice restaurant. The waitress had a noticeably bad attitude. Instead of reacting, I asked her if she was having a rough day. She admitted she was. I simply encouraged her warmly, and from that point on, she treated me like royalty. Kindness turned her day around. Sometimes the dance people want us to engage in with them is their need to be understood.

Of course, we would all prefer people to support our dreams, celebrate our milestones, and be there for us. But what do we do when no one seems to care to help us? We keep dancing anyway. Even those whom God has prompted to assist us may sometimes fail to meet even His expectations.

Often, we're the guilty party because we fantasize about someone's involvement in our endeavors and then become upset when they don't cooperate, but we failed to express our expectations clearly. It's unfair to expect people to know what we want, just because we feel they should know, because of the closeness of the relationship. That doesn't make them bad people. It just means they're humans who need to know what we desire them to do.

In 2000, when I wrote the original version of this book, producing and promoting this book required thousands of dollars—money I didn't have. I asked several people for help, and although they had valid reasons, none were able to contribute financially. That year, I wrote (revised): Even as I write these words, I don't know precisely how God will provide, but I know He will. I believe those individuals support me in prayer, and that's invaluable. I won't waste energy resenting anyone. I need that energy to do what God has called me to do: deliver this message to everyone who needs it.

Celebrate your blessings. *"My life makes its boast in the Lord; let the humble and afflicted hear and be glad"* (Psalm 34:2 AMPC). Not everyone will be happy about what God does in your life. That hurts, especially when you expected them to dance with you. But keep dancing. Eventually someone will join you. And if they don't, praise the Lord anyway. Someone once said, "If you won't praise the Lord, well then, I'll praise Him!"

What are you doing after your brother or sister's dance?

CHAPTER 4:

AFTER THE FRIEND DANCE

Defining Friend

"Friend dance" refers to the moment when someone discovers a true friend.

One day God gave me a definition of *friend* that completely shifted my perspective: *A friend is someone God places in your life to show His love through, and the person allows it.* That definition was so clear and convicting that I had to go back and reconsider those I had previously labeled as friends. A few names on my "friends list" got a quiet minus sign beside them that day. Some people are good-hearted. Some are fun. But a true friend is more than that: They're a vessel of God's love, and they let Him use them.

In today's world, people are more selective about who they label as a *friend*. It's common to hear someone say, "Oh, she's an associate of mine," rather than endearing someone as a friend. That's because the word *friend* has become sacred. An associate may share a workspace with you, but we often share our lives with our friends. A true friend is someone you *want* to trust on every level. That doesn't mean you always *can*, but that deep desire is what defines the connection.

But what happens when someone proves to be untrustworthy? The result is pain. Hurt. Disappointment. You can forgive them—and you should—but does that mean you have to trust them again at the same level? Not necessarily. True friends will rebuild that trust, but it takes time. Keep this in mind: One day, intentionally or not, you may fail someone's trust too, and when that day comes, you'll desire their mercy.

> *Blessed (happy, to be envied, and spiritually prosperous—with life-joy and satisfaction in God's favor and salvation, regardless of their outward conditions) are the merciful, for they shall obtain mercy!*
>
> Matthew 5:7 AMPC

Why Not Many Friends

The Bible also says, *"A man that hath friends must show himself friendly…"* but that's only the first half of the verse. Maurice Graves, one of my cousins, once pointed out what the Amplified Classic Version says in full, and it changed how I read it:

> *The man of many friends [a friend of all the world] will prove himself a bad friend, but there is a friend who sticks closer than a brother.*
>
> Proverbs 18:24 AMPC

That verse may surprise you, especially if you've always thought having a lot of friends meant you were doing something right. But God never called us to please everybody. Even He doesn't try to please everyone. He remains perfect—whether we're pleased with Him or not—and He's still the greatest friend we'll ever have.

God didn't design or intend for us to build close friendships with everyone we meet. Trying to do that will stretch you until you reach your limit. Emotional and social burnout is not the will of God. A healthier principle is simple: Treat others the way you want to be treated. You might hesitate with that because it leaves you vulnerable. Maybe someone's already taken advantage of your kindness. Possibly, you've been there, offering nothing but genuine care, only to be met with mistreatment. That hurts. And that's real.

Let me mention something that may be a revelation to you. The devil has a way of causing your loved ones to become consumed with their own problems. When this happens, it becomes nearly impossible for them to notice your need for attention or concern. They're so overwhelmed by their struggles that they have very little, if any, compassion left to give to anyone else. If you examine yourself honestly, you may discover—as I did—that you've been guilty of this same kind of selfishness at some point.

> *Bear (endure, carry) one another's burdens and troublesome moral faults, and in this way fulfill and observe perfectly the law of Christ (the Messiah) and complete what is lacking [in your obedience to it].*
>
> Galatians 6:2 AMPC

Problems can drain the compassion right out of a person. They become so weak and disheartened that they feel incapable of bearing their own burdens, let alone someone else's. But even in that state, healing is possible. The best response is not criticism; it's intercession.

> *Confess to one another therefore your faults (your slips, your false steps, your offenses, your sins) and pray [also] for one another, that you may be healed and restored [to a spiritual tone of mind and heart].*
>
> James 5:16 AMPC

There are people who, tragically, have grown to hate others, not because they started that way but because they once treated people with fairness and kindness and weren't treated the same in return. They didn't need a lot of people. One genuine friend would've meant the world to them. But time after time, the ones they trusted failed to be true friends. Have you ever experienced that? It does happen. And yes, it hurts.

David knew this kind of pain deeply and desired to escape from it all.

> *And I say, Oh, that I had wings like a dove! I would fly away and be at rest.*
>
> Psalm 55:6 AMPC

I've felt that way more than once, wishing I could escape, start over somewhere new, and leave all the pain behind.

Have you ever found yourself becoming self-centered, not because that's who you are but because it's who life's disappointments have shaped you into? You think, *Why am I like this? I didn't use to be this way.* But you can pinpoint the cause. It's sad, but it's real. *Nobody seems to care. I've sown love, but I'm reaping pain.*

You start noticing things. The person who used to smile warmly now won't even make eye contact. The one you helped financially, time and again, now treats you like you're invisible. The one who once called you a friend never seems to have time for you anymore.

So, again, let us obey God's Word and pray for one another.

Please don't try to buy someone's friendship. If you're able to help someone financially, do it as an act of love, but don't expect it to automatically create a true friendship. I'm always extra careful about assisting people with financial needs until I learn more about their plans to move forward confidently into a stable economic situation. It's also important to me to ask if they faithfully give tithes and offerings to their church, because if they don't, God may be withholding His blessings from them, which could be contributing to their financial difficulty. I don't want to help when my assistance is in direct opposition to an act of God. Once I've asked enough questions, a friendship from a financial transaction is unlikely to materialize.

You may have heard people say, "I don't have any friends. Jesus is my only Friend." Most of the time, people have been deeply hurt by those who say such things. They may call others associates—if that's the case. So, how do we handle that? How do we minister to people like them? Be a friend to them. Friendship is ministry.

Let God show His love to them through you. Everyone needs a friend. Yes, Jesus is our most faithful Friend, but He also desires to bless us with human friendships that reflect His heart. Friendship is good. It helps. It heals. It nurtures. It's real. And there are enough genuine people in the world to choose from. You don't have to walk through life without a friend.

Here's what I've come to believe: Because I've given my life to God and live for Him, He's responsible for taking care of me. After all, He's the One holding my life now. I no longer possess it.

More importantly, He promised to care for me. That's why I'm sharing this with you. If you've surrendered your life to God and you trust Him, then He'll take care of you, too. And once you know He's caring for you, your spirit will feel free to minister friendship to others.

There's a common phrase in Christian circles: *Take care of God's business, and He'll take care of yours.* It may sound simple, but it holds a powerful truth. You don't have to beg Him to care for you. He already said He would.

> *Casting the whole of your care [all your anxieties, all your worries, all your concerns, once and for all] on Him, for He cares for you affectionately and cares about you watchfully.*
>
> 1 Peter 5:7 AMPC

He wants to take care of you. Be a friend, and you will have a friend. God will see to that. It will happen. Be encouraged.

When you've found a friend, the question then becomes, What are you doing after the dance, friend?

CHAPTER 5:

AFTER THE GRADUATION DANCE

The "graduation dance" refers to the milestone of someone completing a significant phase of education.

I can't say I'm especially proud of my academic track record. I did well in grade school. I attended Holy Trinity Catholic School in Orangeburg, South Carolina, where the administration even considered promoting me from kindergarten to the third grade. Thankfully, my parents said no—and now I'm glad they did. Middle school was a mixed experience, with both excellent and not-so-great grades. In high school at Orangeburg-Wilkinson, I earned average grades. Sometimes I made the honor roll. Other times I didn't.

Roll your works upon the Lord [commit and trust them wholly to Him; He will cause your thoughts to become agreeable to His will, and] so shall your plans be established and succeed.

Proverbs 16:3 AMPC

Let me pause to speak directly to high schoolers and those getting ready for it: Please take your education seriously. Study. Prepare. Give it your best. I say this from experience, and I'll walk you through my journey so you can see why.

Before I was born, my parents knew something was different about me. After my mom and dad had their first child, my older sister, Vickey Annette, my Mom's doctor said she wouldn't conceive again because of her anemic condition. But I came along. While she was pregnant with me, someone from a Methodist church she attended gave her a word of prophecy, saying, "That child in your womb is anointed."

I was overdue and born with asthma, but God healed me years ago. Praise God from whom all blessings flow!

I always wanted to be a preacher. Growing up, I constantly received prophecies that confirmed my calling. I used to tell my elementary school friends that I would be a preacher one day. I shared the gospel with them regularly; some of them even came to church with me. From an early age, I knew that I would spend my life preaching. That goal shaped my entire outlook on the future.

High school prepared me for the realities of life. Just the thought of graduation thrilled me. I couldn't wait to "cut a step" (dance) when the day finally came. But after the dance, I had no idea what was ahead.

When the Plan Isn't Yours

Since I have known that God called me to preach, I wanted to attend a Bible college. Specifically, I had my heart set on Rhema Bible Training Center in Tulsa, Oklahoma. But my father didn't want me to go there. It wasn't that he didn't believe in Rhema; he just wanted me to major in business management at Claflin College, right there in Orangeburg. My father had recently retired as Claflin's head chef, so the school held a special significance for him. Unwillingly, I went along with his plan.

My father meant well, and majoring in business management turned out to be a wise choice, especially considering the work I do today. Still, I always encourage young people to follow the dreams God places in their hearts. Parents, support your child's aspirations for their future. God, the One who made them, has already wired them with a desire to prosper. Your job is to pray that He fine-tunes that desire to align with His will, not to replace it with your plan.

Please don't force your child to live out your dream. If they need your pressure to get started, they'll keep needing pressure to keep going. That kind of stress wears on everyone involved, you and your child. Young people need love and encouragement—a lot of it, more than we may realize. Life already brings enough stress without the pressure to be what someone else wants you to be. Trust me. I've been there.

At Claflin, I was elected Freshman Class Chaplain with over ninety percent of the vote. I even made the honor roll a few times. But I still didn't want to be there. No offense, Panthers and Pantherettes—I just knew Bible college was where I was supposed to be.

Eventually, my sister, Arturette, convinced me to attend Orangeburg-Calhoun Technical College. She said, "If you major in nursing, you can get a job anywhere." That sounded good to me, so I enrolled and chose nursing as my major. At first, I was genuinely interested. I did well. But that still wasn't what I wanted. I stayed at O-C Tech and switched my major to respiratory therapy, partly because I had a personal connection, having grown up with asthma. I enjoyed the courses and performed well for a while. But then I failed a class. They told me I'd have to wait an entire year before I could retake it. I felt like I was stuck on a merry-go-round, and I got off. I dropped out.

I found a job at a wholesale warehouse. It was hard labor, physically and emotionally. Some of my high school classmates, now college graduates, were showing up at the warehouse as customers. The embarrassment was absolute.

So, let the part of my story that I just shared speak directly to you. Yes, I had my graduation "dance," but after the dance… well, you see how that went. My inconsistency in applying myself to any of the courses I took is why I'm so passionate about what happens after the celebration ends for you, in every area of your life.

The Value of Correction

> 11 My son, do not despise or shrink from the chastening of the Lord [His correction by punishment or by subjection to suffering or trial]; neither be weary of or impatient about or loathe or abhor His reproof,
> 12 For whom the Lord loves He corrects, even as a father corrects the son in whom he delights.
>
> Proverbs 3:11–12 AMPC

Learn from my correction, not just my mistakes. You see, it's one thing to know what went wrong. It's another thing to know how to fix it. Knowing the correction—that's what helps you grow. So ask yourself: How would you have corrected my situation? Now focus on that.

I wish I had encouraged myself more back then. I wish I had talked to my father again and pleaded with him to let me follow my heart to Bible college. I believe he would've supported me if I had been clearer and more persistent. That right there might've been the correction I needed. I'm just now realizing that as I write this! I'm convinced of this: God works all things together for good.

If you're in high school now, or on your way, prayerfully plan now for what's next. You'll be glad you did. And even if your life choices alter your path, God can reshape your plan into what His will is for your life. Just don't plan without prayer. That's the ultimate key to success. You may already have a dream in your heart, but prayer will help you see it through God's eyes. He knows your limits. He knows your pressure points. And by His Spirit, He'll help you see yourself clearly and make decisions that align with His will.

Now that you've had your graduation dance…what are you doing after the dance?

CHAPTER 6:

DECISION BRINGS DESTINY TO THE DANCE

There is a way which seems right to a man and appears straight before him, but at the end of it is the way of death.

Proverbs 14:12 AMPC

5 Lean on, trust in, and be confident in the Lord with all your heart and mind and do not rely on your own insight or understanding.
6 In all your ways know, recognize, and acknowledge Him, and He will direct and make straight and plain your paths.

Proverbs 3:5–6 AMPC

The T.I.D.A.R. Effect
Time introduces influence.
Influence causes a decision.
Decision fathers every action.
Every action renders a result.

Decision is a powerful force. It's so powerful that only one thing can cancel it: another decision. If you decide to go to the mall, the only thing that can undo that choice is a decision not to go. That's how serious the power of decision is. Destiny, simply put, is what will happen. Therefore, all things being equal, whatever you decide is what will happen.

We make decisions every day of our lives. From the moment we're born until the moment we die, we are making choices. Everything you've done—every move you've made—started as a decision. You're reading this book because of a decision. Whether it was rubbing your nose or attending college, you did it or didn't do it based on a decision you made.

Maybe you've made a decision that made you proud. Have you decided to become a better steward of the money God has given to you? Perhaps you've decided to lose weight. Maybe you've decided to give your heart and soul to the Lord. Maybe your decision was to get married. But whatever the case, can you live with the result of your decision?

In the last chapter, I shared a portion of my academic journey. Regardless of the outcome, I had to live with the results of my decisions. Not all of the results made me happy, but I had to adapt. I've learned that even when our decisions don't yield favorable results, the lessons we learn from making choices can become wisdom that we can apply indefinitely.

We can all attest to the fact that time brings many influences into our lives. The old saying goes, "Birds of a feather flock together." People have a way of influencing our every action. That's why so many motivational speakers urge us to surround ourselves with positive thinkers. They understand the power of the environment. Your surroundings shape your mindset. If you're not careful, they will shape your choices. Don't fall into the "misery loves company" trap. People are easily drawn into atmospheres filled with fear, doubt, or laziness, and they don't even realize it. Whoever or whatever is around you influences you in some way. That influence sets the tone for your decisions. Those decisions will then give birth to your actions. Your actions, in turn, deliver results—good or bad—all of which originate from your surroundings.

When I was growing up, my parents consistently listened to, purchased, and sang gospel music throughout the house. That environment shaped me. The gospel artists I loved then are still my favorites today. When they release new music, I'm eager to hear it and can hardly wait for radio announcers to play their latest songs. While some Christians listen to other genres of music, my surroundings influenced my personal preference for music. Gospel music has been my choice since childhood.

When the Bible says to acknowledge God in all your ways, that includes your decision-making, especially when multiple influences are trying to guide you.

In all your ways know, recognize, and acknowledge Him, and He will direct and make straight and plain your paths.

Proverbs 3:6 AMPC

Learning God's way helps you recognize the right way. His timing becomes your timing. His decisions become your decisions. When that's your posture, you'll succeed.

At the time of this book's earliest release in 2000, I was still waiting on the Lord to bring into full view the evangelistic ministry I strongly desired, and I decided to agree to God's will. I knew I couldn't anoint and launch myself. I couldn't give myself spiritual gifts. Only God could open that door, and I want to walk through it when I can receive the full benefit of what He's prepared.

So, how should we decide? We decide by embracing every influence that comes from God and rejecting every influence that comes from satan. We know the difference between right and wrong, and when we're unsure, we can ask ourselves, "What would Jesus do?" Each decision is a declaration of our destiny.

Now that you understand the power of decision, what will you do after making the right one? Will you act on it? And once your action produces a result, what comes next? If you made a godly decision, be careful not to cancel it by making another decision that opposes it. Only a new decision can undo a previous one. Just as the first one did, the most recent decision will also prompt action. That action will yield a result, and that result will remain in effect until you decide otherwise.

People will usually ask this question: "Will I be successful?" My answer is not complex: Yes, if you decide to be successful, you will be successful. It's essential to recognize that success encompasses more than merely having a substantial amount of money. Success is making the correct decisions and sticking to them. That's true success.

Not all encounters are the results of decisions we've made. Some occurrences arise as our lives unfold, based on the decisions of others that affect our lives. Still, we can shape those situations through prayer. When we pray to discover what the Father already wants to give us, we will receive it when we pray accordingly. Submitting to God's will and having patience are keys to enjoying fulfilled prayers.

My family realized our house was too small for our needs. I prayed that my parents would buy a larger home, but that wasn't what God had in mind. Instead, Prophet Brian Mosley came to our home for dinner and prophesied later that he saw an addition being built onto our house. My parents then decided to expand our existing home, adding four bedrooms plus one and a half bathrooms. I prayed throughout the entire process that the work would be successful, and it was. Virtually, every time the contractor needed materials, they would be on sale. When the addition was complete, my parents had spent less than half of what they had expected. GLORY BE TO GOD!!!

If we ask God what His plans are, He will answer us, although the answer might not be immediate. He doesn't always speak the same way every time, so ask the Holy Spirit to help you become more sensitive to His voice and leading. When you receive His answer, pray into it by asking God to order your steps according to His answer, will, and way. When you follow these steps, you'll walk right into the future God has planned for you. Praise God—His Spirit truly guides us into all truth (John 16:13).

Suppose you've decided to wake up and pray every morning at 5:00 AM. What influences might you allow into your life that would tempt you to undo that decision? Remember, decisions declare your destiny. A decision preceded every action you've ever taken.

So often we may have asked ourselves, "Why do I keep doing wrong?" Because we've decided to. "Why can't I just live holy?" Because we haven't decided to live a holy life. The truth is, knowing the right decision to make is usually simple. The hard part is making the decision and adhering to it. A decision leads to action, and an action proves that a decision has been made.

Money Decisions

Financial needs are made known to the public in various places, not just the church. Yet churches tend to receive the most criticism for sharing their needs through media. Still, millions of dollars are invested faithfully in ministries worldwide. Do you personally support a specific ministry?

Tithes and offerings are commands from God. Malachi, Chapter 3, teaches that principle. Do you give tithes and offerings faithfully to your church? If you don't faithfully attend a local fellowship, please consider doing so, as you will be missing out on incredible experiences, and they will be missing out on the blessings that you can offer. If we don't do anything for God with faithfulness, it doesn't please Him.

> *But without faith it is impossible to please and be satisfactory to Him. For whoever would come near to God must [necessarily] believe that God exists and that He is the rewarder of those who earnestly and diligently seek Him [out].*
>
> Hebrews 11:6 AMPC

Believe it or not, one hundred percent of our money belongs to God, not just ten percent plus an offering. That's why we need to understand what it means to be a steward. A steward is a manager, and we are all managers over God's money and everything else He places in our hands. If we handle what He gives us in a way that pleases Him, He'll entrust us with more. Jesus shared a parable that teaches this very principle.

> *20 And so he that had received five talents came and brought other five talents, saying, Lord, thou deliveredst unto me five talents: behold, I have gained beside them five talents more.*
> *21 His lord said unto him, Well done, thou good and faithful servant: thou hast been faithful over a few things, I will make thee ruler over many things: enter thou into the joy of thy lord.*
> *22 He also that had received two talents came and said, Lord, thou deliveredst unto me two talents: behold, I have gained two other talents beside them.*
> *23 His lord said unto him, Well done, good and faithful servant; thou hast been faithful over a few things, I will make thee ruler over many things: enter thou into the joy of thy lord.*
>
> Matthew 25:20–23 KJV

Let's take a moment to talk about tithes. I believe media, especially television, has helped many outreach ministries expand on a national and international level. I financially support some of these ministries. Still, if you're a member of a local church, direct your tithes and offerings there first, according to Malachi 3. Even if you're connected to global ministries, your local church should not be neglected. That's the congregation of believers God has assigned to walk with you, pray with you, and guide you. It's a matter of honor.

Now let's look at offerings. Someone once asked, "How do I know how much to give?" Tithing is simple; it's ten percent (10%) of your income. But offerings are led by the Spirit. They're tied to the level of harvest God wants to bring into your life. God is the One Who gives increase to the seeds we obediently plant. I give at least 13% of my income as tithes and offerings to my local church, and I provide additional donations to other ministries as God leads me to do so.

> *I planted, Apollos watered, but God [all the while] was making it grow and [He] gave the increase.*
>
> 1 Corinthians 3:6 AMPC

God knows the size of the blessing He prepared for us, so He instructs us on which size seed is needed to produce His planned blessing. Perhaps you're comfortable giving $15. But if the Holy Spirit prompts you to donate $200, it's because that size seed is necessary to receive what He's preparing for you to receive—something greater than what a $15 seed would produce. We only give by faith and out of strict obedience to God's commands. Don't hesitate. Remember:

> *For as the human body apart from the spirit is lifeless, so faith apart from [its] works of obedience is also dead.*
>
> James 2:26 AMPC

If God stirs your heart to give to a ministry, give what He asks of you. It won't go unnoticed by Him. Just be sure that your giving flows from joy and obedience. Giving tithes without offerings is still disobedience. God does not honor disobedience.

If God can't trust us to give, He can't trust us to receive. If we don't trust God with our outgo, we can't expect to trust Him for our income. He must be in complete control of our finances. He will bless us with ideas, creativity, and increase, but we must never forget who gave us the power to prosper.

> *But you shall [earnestly] remember the Lord your God, for it is He Who gives you power to get wealth, that He may establish His covenant which He swore to your fathers, as it is this day.*
> Deuteronomy 8:18 AMPC

I've heard countless testimonies of believers who gave in obedience and received unexpected financial miracles. I'm sure you have testimonials as well. Reflect on those moments as reminders of God's faithfulness. No one can build your faith like you can when you remember what He's already done.

Have you ever decided not to give when God prompted you to donate? What made you choose not to give? There are certain words and phrases that demons know will discourage us from obeying God. Their job is to keep those and other selfish thoughts circling in our minds until they convince us not to give. Whatever the enemy—whether it is the devil, demons, imps, evil spirits, evil powers, or principalities speaking to us, if we listen and act on it, those demonic spirits will use those words against us repeatedly, keeping us bound, disobedient, and not in line to receive God's blessings.

Our evil enemies will conquer us if we don't conquer them. Maybe you've heard something like, "You gave a $100 bill in that church service last week and didn't get anything for it." Or "Do you believe that giving money will cause something good to happen for you?" These statements aim to short-circuit our faith in God that He will keep His promise and bless us for being obedient in our giving. Don't let the enemy deceive you. Giving unlocks something spiritual. It opens the windows of Heaven for God to pour out a blessing.

What are you allowing to influence your decision on giving? Think about that honestly.

> *Give, and [gifts] will be given to you; good measure, pressed down, shaken together, and running over, will they pour into [the pouch formed by] the bosom [of your robe and used as a bag]. For with the measure you deal out [with the measure you use when you confer benefits on others], it will be measured back to you.*
>
> Luke 6:38 AMPC

If giving is just an occasional event in our lives, then receiving will also be an occasional event. But if giving becomes our lifestyle, receiving will follow suit. Is generosity an occasional act or a lifelong commitment for you? We'll never become obedient givers according to God's will until we decide to live generously.

Many church members are deeply committed to giving. I've seen it. They sacrifice joyfully. I've watched them testify of God's blessings—sometimes financial, sometimes not. Still, they declare, "I'm blessed and highly favored!" They aren't saying that because they always get something tangible in return. They say it because they know Who their Source is—God, our loving and caring Father.

Not all giving is material, and not all receiving is either. You might give your time and gain a true friend in return. You could comfort someone who's struggling, and they might feel compelled to bless you by paying a bill on your behalf.

Living in a world that's often selfish and ungrateful, we must still choose to give to others what God commands—a fight of faith—and it's a fight God has called us to finish. We're in a war to destroy evil works, not just to bruise it (1 John 3:8). The devil is fighting to eliminate every trace of good. But when we rise with the strength of God's goodness, this world will see and say with confidence, "Good conquers evil!"

Some wait on God to cause them to win a sweepstakes (of course, that *can* happen). Many people want to find money or receive blessings without putting in any effort, which is highly unlikely to occur. Yes, God can create nontraditional streams of wealth for us, but we must remain open to every way God may choose to bless us.

Pray to know the mind of God—His intended pathways for you to receive the specific blessings you desire. The blessings we believe God will provide *are* possible, according to His will and way.

What about those who don't give and still appear prosperous? Their riches will soon come to an end. Be encouraged to have faith in God, not in the hope of attaining what others have. That aspiration is a demonic scheme to infiltrate our hearts with covetousness, desiring what others have (Exodus 20:17).

> *Wealth [not earned but] won in haste or unjustly or from the production of things for vain or detrimental use [such riches] will dwindle away, but he who gathers little by little will increase [his riches].*
>
> Proverbs 13:11 AMPC

> *The wealth of the sinner [finds its way eventually] into the hands of the righteous, for whom it was laid up.*
>
> Proverbs 13:22 AMPC

Decisions Made from Fear

> *For God did not give us a spirit of timidity (of cowardice, of craven and cringing and fawning fear), but [He has given us a spirit] of power and of love and of calm and well-balanced mind and discipline and self-control.*
>
> 2 Timothy 1:7 AMPC

Kenneth Copeland once said, "Faith is believing that something is going to happen. Fear is believing that something is going to happen." What do we choose to believe—the positive or the negative?

If we feel fear while trying to trust God, it doesn't always mean we're afraid. Often, we're only sensing the *presence* of the spirit of fear. To *fear* is to accept the fear and act on its influence. But we don't have to take it.

Someone once told an untruth about me, and a meeting was scheduled to address the issue. I knew what it was about, and I could feel the demon of fear trying to convince me to respond in fear. I rejected it—over and over—because I knew God would fight for me.

> *The Lord will fight for you, and you shall hold your peace and remain at rest.*
>
> Exodus 14:14 AMPC

I prayed and encouraged myself with the Word of God. The meeting went in my favor, and the other party was reprimanded.

Why live in fear when God is in control? The fear of the Lord is the beginning of wisdom—not the kind of fear that paralyzes but reverence that empowers. It's a deep respect for the sovereignty of God.

I recall watching a behind-the-scenes making of a movie on TV. The announcer said something that struck me: "A man in a hurry fears time." That's precisely why many people don't see the full manifestation of God's promises: They think He's taking too long.

We want results before we feel we've run out of time. But God owns time. He doesn't take time; He uses it. He commands it. He causes time to work in your favor when you remain in His will. Don't panic. Don't worry. Don't fear. Just believe. God is never late. Fear not. Only believe.

When I was in my twenties, I ventured into a business. I wanted to write, compose, and sell jingles—the little songs that advertise a product or service. I spent hundreds of dollars on phone calls and books about music in advertising. I found a program that promised significant results, and the company convinced me that if I didn't get it right away, I'd never break into the business. I couldn't afford the cost, but I tried everything I could to raise the money. When I couldn't get it, I was deeply discouraged. That's when God told me to stop trying to squeeze through the cracks—and wait for Him to open the door. And He did—in His time, not mine.

Eventually, I wrote a jingle for A. L. Williams Insurance Company. They accepted it for promotional use only. I didn't get paid, but they agreed to use it exclusively on their in-house satellite channel. It wasn't aired commercially; the company aired it during the closing credits of one of their internal training sessions. Even so, it reached throughout the United States, the Virgin Islands, Canada, and other countries. I was featured in the local newspaper. That free opportunity led to writing, recording, and selling my jingles to other companies.

God can take as much time as He wants because He owns time. If we give Him control of the situation, there will always be time. He'll make sure of it. But if He's waiting on you to do your part, then time might start working against you. If you've obeyed what He's asked of you, then just wait. When He has something for you to do, He will give you enough time to do it. God has all the time He needs—because He *has* time!

"Well, Shane," someone might say, "they're coming to repossess my property *tomorrow*." What did God say to you specifically? "He said everything is going to be all right." Then trust Him. Examine the fear you feel. Does it stem from that word "tomorrow"? God holds tomorrow just as securely as He holds today. This trial might just be a test of your trust in Him.

God's time should be our time, no matter what time it is! He's not anxious, and if we belong to Him, we don't need to be worried either. Wait and see. Wait on the Lord, and you *will* see His salvation. Time has to obey Him concerning you. If God is in control of your situation, then time is working in your favor. Why fear what God controls? Talk about living worry-free! Live with the assurance that your times are in His hands.

> *My times are in Your hands; deliver me from the hands of my foes and those who pursue me and persecute me.*
>
> Psalm 31:15 AMPC

Never forget: Without faith, it is impossible to please God. If we take the situation out of His care and try to solve it our way, we'll consider ourselves running out of time. Then, knowing how humans react to highly stressful moments, we'll run directly back to God to plead for His mercy. When we surrender our situations to Him and faithfully leave them in His care, He'll secure, restore, and replace them with the success He originally had in mind for us.

Be patient. Wait on the Lord. Passing time may be your best friend. Remember my jingle business? I let time pass while believing God's Word, and the blessings came!

> *So also faith, if it does not have works (deeds and actions of obedience to back it up), by itself is destitute of power (inoperative, dead)..*
>
> James 2:17 AMPC

Waiting is an act of faith. It's an action. When someone tells you they're coming to see you, what do you do? You wait. You trust their word, so you take action; you stay available. That's what faith with works looks like. Faith without works is unresponsive. But faith with works is alive and gets the job done. Works are the actions faith produces. If you genuinely believe, you'll respond. The choice is yours. Will you respond to what God has said—or ignore it?

This lesson is how the Holy Spirit taught me the reality and power of faith with works. It's my prayer that you now understand it better as well. The "works" always stem from your decision. So let me ask you: What will you do with what God has said? Just remember: You will only ever do what you have decided to do.

What Will You Decide?

Why do people change? Their decisions change. Someone might remember you as mean or short-tempered, but if they see a new, gentler you, they'll wonder what happened. Just tell them—you changed your decisions. Perhaps you once lived paycheck to paycheck, complaining about life, but now you're living prosperously. You made better decisions, and God honored them. You didn't just get better; you *decided* to be better. And your decision led to the actions that ultimately produced your breakthrough.

We can't do something else until we *decide* on something else.

Make the decision to give your whole life to God and God alone. Make the decision never to walk away from Him. Decide to live in obedience to His will. Decide to hear and follow the voice of the Holy Spirit. Decide to give everything He asks you to give. Decide to pray. If you can medically do so, decide to fast.

Decide to read your Bible every day. Decide to do what is right. Decide to listen to and obey what God declares through your pastor. Decide to decide!

And after you've made the decision, now what? What are you doing after the decision dance?

CHAPTER 7:
AFTER THE SOCIETY DANCE

The society dance refers to the process by which society accepts someone.

> *Woe to (alas for) you when everyone speaks fairly and handsomely of you and praises you, for even so their forefathers did to the false prophets.*
>
> Luke 6:26 AMPC

The late Bishop F. D. Washington responded to this verse both jokingly and insightfully: "Woe unto you if no one speaks well of you." Everyone wants to be socially accepted. But when we're not, fear can creep in—the fear that we'll be rejected, especially by the ones we long to be embraced by.

This fear is a common struggle for preachers' kids. Many of them desperately want to be accepted for who they truly are. But if society doesn't affirm them, they often feel pressure to change, becoming more like the crowd that draws them in. Why? Because they just want to be accepted.

But if becoming like society pulls you away from your relationship with God, it's not worth it. It's forbidden. My prayer is that each of us would discover our place in God and allow Him to position us, not society. Only what we do for Christ will last. Everything else will eventually collapse.

Who Is Society?

The Bible doesn't use the word "society" or "social," but for the sake of this chapter, let's define society as *all people, collectively, as a community of interdependent individuals governed by influence.* So again, who is this society we feel so pressured to please?

The truth is, society is us. The media has significantly shaped much of society, influencing its standards of what is acceptable and what is not. The unspoken rule seems to be "Give the people what they want," and if you challenge that, society calls you outdated or irrelevant. If they like you, you're "in." If not, you're "out."

If society expects you to marry within your race, and you do, society will praise you. But if you don't, you may be labeled unacceptable. And yet, others in society say that marrying outside your race is completely fine. It's divided, conflicted, and imperfect.

Social well-being has been defined as *the ability to cope successfully with society*, but true social well-being only comes by making the right decisions—God-pleasing decisions. As long as God is pleased, don't lose sleep over whether anyone else is. You'll never satisfy everyone.

Bishop Ronald E. Brown once said, "Please God, and those who are worth being pleased will be pleased." That's one of the best definitions of true social well-being I've ever heard.

Will Pleasing Society Reward You?

Most people believe that if they successfully please society, the rewards are imminent. However, some of the most miserable individuals are those who have tried to change who they are just to gain acceptance. That reward wasn't worth the cost. There's a real danger in making social acceptance more important than God's acceptance. We, the saints of God, are not of this world.

> *They are not of the world (worldly, belonging to the world), [just] as I am not of the world.*
>
> John 17:16 AMPC

Society did not fully accept Jesus when He was on Earth, and many still don't accept Him.

> *For in Him we live and move and have our being...*
>
> Acts 17:28 KJV

Because of our commitment to Jesus, society won't fully accept us either. But who cares? Just give me Jesus. That's not arrogance; it's clarity. Some will wholeheartedly receive Jesus, but many won't. Still, God gave us a mission to share Jesus with everyone we can. Then, the world has a choice—faith or fate.

> *15 And He said to them, Go into all the world and preach and publish openly the good news (the Gospel) to every creature [of the whole human race].*
>
> *16 He who believes [who adheres to and trusts in and relies on the Gospel and Him Whom it sets forth] and is baptized will be saved [from the penalty of eternal death]; but he who does not believe [who does not adhere to and trust in and rely on the Gospel and Him Whom it sets forth] will be condemned.*
>
> Mark 16:15–16 AMPC

If you haven't given your life to the Lord, now is the time. God wants to save you through His only begotten Son, Jesus Christ. God did not create the everlasting fire of eternal torment as punishment for you; He prepared it for the devil and his angels.

> *Then He will say to those at His left hand, Begone from Me, you cursed, into the eternal fire prepared for the devil and his angels!*
>
> Matthew 25:41 AMPC

The prayer for salvation is located at the end of this book; yet, I now sense that the Holy Spirit wants me to place it here. If you don't know Jesus Christ, the Messiah, as Savior and Lord, or need to renew your relationship with Him, please use the following words to speak to God now, even if it's in a whisper. He's waiting for you:

Father God, I come before You now in the name of Jesus Christ. I confess that I am a sinner. Please forgive me and save me from all of my past sins. I know Jesus Christ is Your Son, Who died for my sins, and that You raised Him from the dead. Jesus, I invite You into my heart right now. Come in and live Your life through me so that I can please our Father just as You please our Father. I now believe that You have come into my heart and life. Father, I have asked and prayed for all these things in the name of Jesus Christ. Thank You for saving me and freeing me from the power of every devil. Father, I have given You my life. I no longer have it. I will live for You and You alone! In Jesus Christ's name, I pray, Amen! I AM SAVED!

GLORY BE TO GOD!!! You are saved! Thank you for taking this step to help society more than before by sharing with them what you've just experienced. Because we don't want anyone we know or meet to be cast into the eternal lake of fire, we will witness for Jesus and testify about our relationship with Him daily. Please share what Jesus has done for you with those who don't yet know Him, as well as with those who do and need a reminder and encouragement.

Are You Socially Accepted?

You may feel accepted as a Christian. Maybe you're not a Christian at all and still feel accepted. Perhaps you've simply decided to ignore society's quiet rejections. Or maybe your love for people runs so deeply that you hardly notice when someone rejects you. Or perhaps you just don't care. Either way, you feel accepted.

I want to take a moment to honor street preachers. I respect them deeply. People mock, dismiss, and ignore them, yet they continue to proclaim the truth of God's Word. Jesus has saved many lost souls because of their bold obedience. May God continue to bless each of them.

Acceptance, in many ways, is a mindset. Some people interpret rejection as just "normal life with a few bumps." To them, this phrase defines acceptance. They're aware that society perceives their worship, diet, and lifestyle as different, and they're comfortable with that. They believe society accepts differences. They refuse to deny their God to feel a sense of social inclusion.

I have a similar example. It took place when I attended Claflin College. One of the people I shared the saving message of Jesus Christ with said something that stirred me. They didn't want to accept Jesus into their life at that time, but they said to someone (concerning me), "I think that it is beautiful what he is doing. It just isn't for me." That individual in society accepted what I was doing, but sadly, he rejected the idea of becoming involved in a relationship with Jesus. I didn't let that rest there. I continued to plant seeds of inspiration in that individual prayerfully.

Even those who have not yet found Christ may very well know they need the Lord in their lives. Yet, they maintain friendships with both Christians and non-Christians because they feel accepted by both.

> *You [are like] unfaithful wives [having illicit love affairs with the world and breaking your marriage vow to God]! Do you not know that being the world's friend is being God's enemy? So whoever chooses to be a friend of the world takes his stand as an enemy of God.*
>
> James 4:4 AMPC

If You Do Not Feel Socially Accepted, Why?

Some feel their lifestyle is appalling to everyone around them. Many remain stuck in the shame of their past. Their history grips their hearts with fear. They carry the humiliation of past behavior and wrestle with low self-esteem so deeply that it feels permanent. Without the miracle of God's steadfast love, that kind of self-loathing never lifts. Some people never feel accepted by anyone, not even their peers.

We must also remember that any lifestyle that contradicts God's Word must end immediately, regardless of whether society accepts it or not. God wants us to enjoy the righteous freedom He offers to every soul afflicted by sin. No matter how bound we feel, if we ask the Lord to free us, He will.

> *So if the Son liberates you [makes you free men], then you are really and unquestionably free.*
>
> John 8:36 AMPC

Jesus will set us free! Amen! It may sound simple, and it's not always easy, but it's indeed possible.

On the other hand, even the lifestyles that please God are sometimes treated as evil by people under the influence of prejudice. That prejudicial demon is the part of society that rejects people who are living in righteousness.

What then shall we say to [all] this? If God is for us, who [can be] against us? [Who can be our foe, if God is on our side?]

Romans 8:31 AMPC

Pray for society. Don't let any demon of prejudice distract you from what God has promised for you and your family. Christian, be bold. Be strong. For the Lord your God is with you!

And David told Solomon his son, Be strong and courageous, and do it. Fear not; be not dismayed. For the Lord God, my God, is with you. He will not fail or forsake you until you have finished all the work for the service of the house of the Lord.

1 Chronicles 28:20 AMPC

Whether you feel accepted or rejected by society, God has a Word for you.

If You Are Accepted—What Now?

Someone once told me the reason some people are obsessed with money is that they always feel the need to prove something. They've always had the best clothes, the best cars, and the most respected circles of friends. If they were to lose it all, they'd feel like they'd lost their place in society. They fear that people would say, "They don't have it anymore." That kind of fear crushes people. If society's acceptance leads you into materialism, you've missed the point.

God gives favor so doors will open—not so we can flaunt what we've gained, but so we can accomplish His will on Earth. He'll lay the foundation. He'll open the way. But the work? That's up to us.

Therefore, my beloved brethren, be firm (steadfast), immovable, always abounding in the work of the Lord [always being superior,

*excelling, doing more than enough in the service of the Lord],
knowing and being continually aware that your labor in the Lord
is not futile [it is never wasted or to no purpose].*

1 Corinthians 15:58 AMPC

To someone unsure of their purpose, "work" sounds intimidating. But without the favor of God, you'll never reach those He's called you to reach. Our assignment is already in place. Proclaim the gospel of Jesus Christ. Speak the truth about heaven and hell.

Therefore, being conscious of fearing the Lord with respect and reverence, we seek to win people over [to persuade them]....

2 Corinthians 5:11 AMPC

What are you doing after the social dance?

CHAPTER 8:

WHEN LONELINESS KEEPS YOU COMPANY

One random evening when I was in my twenties, I was sitting on the floor at the foot of my bed, and I began to think about how lonely I was. I didn't know what to do about it. I just felt so lonely. No one had said or done anything wrong to me. I was just feeling lonely.

Sometimes, everybody shows you love except the one person you strongly desire to receive it from. Have you ever experienced that? People show love, but you only want to be loved by a specific individual. And not only do they refuse to love you, but they also reject your love. Rejection is an awful experience that pierces the emotions.

Deep down, you might even long to be close to the ones who are already trying to love you, but you've rejected them. You know you won't reciprocate their love because you're holding out for someone else. I've been there. That's a state of selfishness that can invite feelings of loneliness. Be fair to yourself—and to others—by being open to true love. As I said earlier, love isn't love until you've given it away.

Back when I was sitting on the floor, the Lord asked me a question. He said, "Isn't it something how loneliness wants to keep you company?" That day, I learned that loneliness is more than just a feeling.

If you're battling loneliness, I want you to know that God can and will set you free. He will give you knowledge, wisdom, and understanding about loneliness—even right here in this chapter. If you're open, the Spirit of God will minister to you.

In the book of Genesis, God made Adam. But then God saw that Adam was alone, and He created Eve. It's essential to note that not everyone feels lonely when they are alone. Often, people prefer to be alone and will fellowship faithfully when the time arises. Other than those times, they're satisfied being alone, and they do not experience loneliness.

For those of us who do battle with loneliness when we're alone, what should we do when loneliness wants to keep us company? We can look to God and let Him fulfill our lives with the ones He prepared for us.

> *Then Adam said, This [creature] is now bone of my bones and flesh of my flesh; she shall be called Woman, because she was taken out of a man.*
>
> Genesis 2:23 AMPC

Eve's presence erased Adam's loneliness. But even when your loneliness is gone, be careful what you do after that celebration.

God has a pattern. He created Adam for Himself. He created Eve for Adam. I believe God created each of us for someone else, not just for ourselves. Is loneliness keeping you company right now? Be encouraged. God has already prepared someone who will fill that void. And when God sends them, never place that person before Him. God must always come first. If you haven't put God first, what you think is loneliness may be a situation He's allowed to draw you closer to Him. God is a jealous God.

> *You shall not bow down yourself to them or serve them; for I the Lord your God am a jealous God...*
>
> Exodus 20:5 AMPC

God wants to be the first to fulfill our lives, just as He was for Adam. He wants our relationship with Him to continue growing, and the opportunity to do so is already here. All we have to do is start talking to Him. He's waiting for us. Don't let the moment of affirmatively responding to His desire for you pass you by.

Why does loneliness show up in your life? Have you put the wrong people in it? God knows who belongs. When you try to take His place by inserting people into your life without His guidance, those same people may eventually frustrate you. Then, you'll want them gone from your life, and loneliness returns.

But when God places someone in your life, all things being equal to God's will, loneliness can't take their place—unless you reject the person He sent or other ungodly factors present themselves. Even more so, loneliness can't affect you unless you invite it. Having company around us is something we invite.

Anyone who barges in uninvited is rude and takes the place of the one who was supposed to be there. That's why a vacancy could be a blessing. If we force the wrong people into our lives, we will push the right ones away. Wait on God. If you do, your joy will be complete. Have faith. Believe—with patience—that God will send the one who is truly bone of your bone and flesh of your flesh. That person may very well have the same God-ordained foundation that you do, made from the exact spiritual blueprint.

> 11 Now when Job's three friends heard of all this evil that was come upon him, they came each one from his own place, Eliphaz the Temanite and Bildad the Shuhite and Zophar the Naamathite, for they had made an appointment together to come to condole with him and to comfort him.
> 12 And when they looked from afar off and saw him [disfigured] beyond recognition, they lifted up their voices and wept; and each one tore his robe, and they cast dust over their heads toward the heavens.
> 13 So they sat down with [Job] on the ground for seven days and seven nights, and none spoke a word to him, for they saw that his grief and pain were very great.
> Job 2:11-13 AMPC

After Job lost almost everything—including all of his children—three of his friends came to comfort him. For seven days and nights, they sat with him in complete silence. Why? Because sometimes, when the weight of grief is too heavy for words, just being there is enough. Our presence alone can create an atmosphere of love that helps our loved ones begin to process their pain.

For many of us, all we need right now is a friend. God knows the exact person who can be that friend. The right friend may not know everything, but they'll be able to handle what we share with them.

I haven't led a complicated life, but I have encountered some unusual experiences. Gospel recording artist Bryan Wilson—my first spiritual son and someone who is more like a biological son—has walked with me through some of my most difficult seasons. I've shared a lot with him, and more often than not, he gets it. He's been a faithful prayer partner and a thoughtful sounding board. I'm grateful to God for the gift of understanding He's given to those He uses to help us in life.

We all need someone who understands us. Even if our confidants don't understand every situation, they can at least understand our viewpoint. They may not agree with everything, but they can still offer loving advice and correction when needed.

God won't give you a friend who pampers you all the time. We need friends who will help us end our pity parties. I thank God for Bryan. Twenty-five years ago, when this book was initially published, I noted that he was the best friend the Lord had given me, next to the Holy Spirit.

"God provides" is an appropriate phrase. God has created the people we need as friends. We don't have to entertain loneliness. Instead of wasting energy on loneliness, reserve your strength for the one God has prepared for you—unless this is the season where He's calling you closer, and just wanting you for Himself. If so, do everything you can to please Him. If you wait on God, He'll send the right person. And remember, custom-made items always take longer to produce than mass-produced ones. So, get rid of loneliness and make room for your blessings.

Say this aloud: "Loneliness, get out! God has someone to take your place! God has the one that I need! God has the one that He has ordained to take your place! I will serve God first, and then I will wait on the Lord and be of good courage. He shall strengthen my heart!"

> *Wait and hope for and expect the Lord; be brave and of good courage and let your heart be stout and enduring. Yes, wait for and hope for and expect the Lord.*
>
> Psalm 27:14 AMPC

Maybe you're thinking, *It's all my fault. I put the wrong one in my life.* But God looks beyond the fault and sees the need. He sees that you invited loneliness only because you were trying to fill a deeper need.

What was that need? Healing? Security? Love? Whatever it was, God wants to heal it. Once He meets the need, the fault disappears. You won't need the wrong person or the feeling of loneliness anymore.

With the *faith-with-works* principle in place, loneliness will flee, and God will provide. It all comes down to faith and action. If you believe God will send the right person, then wait. Waiting is an act of faith, and faith is pleasing to God.

> *But without faith it is impossible to please and be satisfactory to Him. For whoever would come near to God must [necessarily] believe that God exists and that He is the rewarder of those who earnestly and diligently seek Him [out].*
>
> Hebrews 11:6 AMPC

Faith in action fathers miracles. Can you name one thing God has ever done that wasn't miraculous? I can't. Everything He does carries the mark of the miraculous. So when we invite God into our loneliness, we invite a miracle into our space. He will deliver us, but it begins by making Him our priority in life.

And speaking of priority, here's a strong note worth remembering: when the word priority first entered the English language, it was singular. It wasn't until 500 years later that time management experts introduced the plural form—priorities. But God was never meant to share space on a list. He is the priority. Everything and everyone else comes after our devotion to Him. When we focus on being with Him, enjoying His company more than anyone else, and commit to following His lead, He will empower us to fulfill all else He has called us to do.

Now, the question is: What are you going to do with your company after the dance?

CHAPTER 9:

OPTICAL ILLUSIONS

An optical illusion occurs when what you see creates a false perception of reality, either of what you're looking at or where you are.

Have you ever been waiting at a traffic light, and it seemed as if your car was moving forward even though your foot was firmly on the brake? So you applied even more pressure, only to realize that the vehicle next to you was moving backward. Your car hadn't budged. That was an optical illusion.

I've experienced this illusion. After it happened, the Holy Spirit gave me a revelation. He said some people surround themselves with others who make them think they're moving forward. In reality, the ones they're watching are moving backward—and the ones thinking they're moving forward haven't moved at all.

I pray you experience many dances of your own. But be careful with whom you walk closely. Don't let the enemy trick you into putting the wrong person in your life, as we discussed in the last chapter. God does not want us to walk by sight. If we do, we'll fall for the deception of optical illusions. But if we refuse to walk by sight, no one can fool us. We must walk by faith, not by sight.

> *For we walk by faith [we regulate our lives and conduct ourselves by our conviction or belief respecting man's relationship to God and divine things, with trust and holy fervor; thus we walk] not by sight or appearance.*
>
> 2 Corinthians 5:7 AMPC

> *So faith comes by hearing [what is told], and what is heard comes by the preaching [of the message that came from the lips] of Christ (the Messiah Himself).*
>
> Romans 10:17 AMPC

Some people only believe based on what they see. But what they see may be nothing more than an optical illusion. Don't become a believer in false facts and fictional impressions.

Those who walk by sight miss easy opportunities. They stare at the journey instead of the destination, misjudge faces and motives, and confuse identity. They stumble, they fall, and they focus more on the ceiling than the sky. In short, they still can't see everything.

We must walk like the blind walking through unfamiliar territory. The Holy Spirit, Who knows the way, can lead us.

> *For all who are led by the Spirit of God are sons of God.*
>
> Romans 8:14 AMPC

Women, take heart. The word *sons* here refers not to gender but to position. Those who allow God's Spirit to lead them are His children. When people who are blind take each step in confidence based on being led, that's faith with works. It's an action that proves trust, and this pleases God.

> *But without faith it is impossible to please and be satisfactory to Him. For whoever would come near to God must [necessarily] believe that God exists and that He is the rewarder of those who earnestly and diligently seek Him [out].*
>
> Hebrews 11:6 AMPC

> *So also faith, if it does not have works (deeds and actions of obedience to back it up), by itself is destitute of power (inoperative, dead).*
>
> James 2:17 AMPC

...And how can they hear without a preacher?

Romans 10:14 AMPC

God gives us leaders—pastors—to hear Him on our behalf and to guide us. Yes, we can listen to God for ourselves, but we still need shepherds to feed and lead us. Obeying those God has placed over us is another example of faith in action.

Even if a pastor fails in an area of their personal life, they are still God's servants. I'm not talking about personality flaws; I'm talking about the truth they speak. If they declare God's truth, it's still truth, no matter who says it. A pastor I know, Heanon Tate, put it like this: "If a drunk man says, 'Jesus is coming soon,' it's still true."

Let's look at two key scriptures:

For it is not merely hearing the Law [read] that makes one righteous before God, but it is the doers of the Law who will be held guiltless and acquitted and justified.

Romans 2:13 AMPC

For no person will be justified (made righteous, acquitted, and judged acceptable) in His sight by observing the works prescribed by the Law. For [the real function of] the Law is to make men recognize and be conscious of sin [not mere perception, but an acquaintance with sin which works toward repentance, faith, and holy character].

Romans 3:20 AMPC

Romans 2:13 says the doer will be justified. Romans 3:20 states that the deeds of the law will not justify anyone. Is that a contradiction? No. Someone may obey the law legally but still be morally wrong. You can keep a law but hate it in your heart. In other words, you're law-abiding but not righteous. True righteousness only comes when obedience flows from the heart, not just from fear of consequence.

I'll use myself as an example. I usually obey traffic laws. Occasionally, I speed or "buck" at a stop sign. And I know most officers won't pull someone over for going just seven or eight miles per hour above the speed limit. So I set my cruise control right under that limit—not because I want to obey the law but because I don't want a ticket. I want to go faster, but I don't like the penalty. People driving behind me might think I'm a model citizen, but in my heart, I'm trying to pass everybody!

One day, while I was driving, going about 5-7 miles over the speed limit, the Holy Spirit asked me, "If Jesus came back right now, would you go to Heaven?" I looked around at the other cars zooming past me and thought that there would be a lot of people going to hell if speeding was so bad, and I didn't believe that was the case.

I responded, "Yes, I believe I would go to Heaven. Then the Holy Spirit said, "You're doing wrong. You know you're doing wrong, and you're intentionally doing wrong. Would you go to Heaven if Jesus came back right now?" I immediately reduced my speed to the posted speed limit, set my cruise control, and that is still my practice today.

Why do we live a Christian life? Is it because we love the Lord and want to please Him? Or is it just to avoid hell? Many may admire our lives for varying reasons, assuming our dedication is to honor Jesus. But is that true, or are we simply trying to avoid eternal punishment? What's our heart's motive toward Jesus? Do we choose to live for Him out of love? When we do, He will give us life more abundantly.

> *The thief comes only in order to steal and kill and destroy. I came that they may have and enjoy life, and have it in abundance (to the full, till it overflows).*
>
> John 10:10 AMPC

Remember, the only way to be fooled by an optical illusion is to walk by sight. Walk by faith and not by sight—before, during, and after the dance.

CHAPTER 10:

ARE YOU IGNORANT?

My people are destroyed for lack of knowledge; because you [the priestly nation] have rejected knowledge, I will also reject you that you shall be no priest to Me; seeing you have forgotten the law of your God, I will also forget your children.

Hosea 4:6 AMPC

Please don't be offended by the title of this chapter. It will make sense soon. This chapter will help you draw closer to a more intimate relationship with the Father.

Of course, one definition of "ignorant" is "having a lack of knowledge." But here's something I hadn't considered for many years: The word "ignorant" comes from the French word "ignorare," which is also the root of the English word "ignore." To ignore means to deliberately disregard, to pay no attention to, or to refuse to consider. That changes things, doesn't it? The origin of the word "ignorant" reveals that ignorance is often not accidental; it's intentional. Many people lack knowledge because they fail to acquire it. So, are you ignorant because you simply haven't learned the truth yet, or are you ignorant because you've been ignoring the truth?

Why do people ignore the truth? That's the question the Lord asked me one day. And He gave me an insightful answer: People ignore or fail to acquire the truth because they believe they already know it.

What if your neighbor knocks on your door, complaining that your dog destroyed their flowerbed? You're confident your dog couldn't have done it; after all, he's chained in the backyard. You tell your neighbor they must be mistaken, but when the two of you go to investigate, you find your dog broke the chain and escaped. You ignored the truth, not out of stubbornness, but because you thought you already knew the truth.

That's how ignorance works—knowledge produces ability. When we learn how to do something, all things being equal, we can now do it. But what we do with that ability—that's where responsibility comes in. Responsibility is our response to our abilities.

I never used to think of "responsibility" as a compound word, but the Holy Spirit opened my eyes to it in a new way. He truly is the inspiration behind the Word of God—and behind this book.

So, how do you respond to the abilities God has given you? The way you respond determines how well you handle your responsibilities. The Bible is clear:

> *So any person who knows what is right to do but does not do it, to him it is sin.*
>
> James 4:17 AMPC

Sin destroys. If we neglect our responsibility, even though we have the knowledge and ability to act, we open the door to destruction. For example, if we've learned how to protect ourselves during a hurricane, we can also protect others. If you fail to act on that ability, you've neglected your responsibility. And when the storm hits, you'll suffer, not because you were helpless but because you ignored what you knew to do.

> *Therefore let anyone who thinks he stands [who feels sure that he has a steadfast mind and is standing firm], take heed lest he fall [into sin].*
>
> 1 Corinthians 10:12 AMPC

If you do what you're supposed to do, you're considered to be standing. So, is it a sin to think that you stand? No. In this verse, God instructs those who believe they are standing. "Take heed" is a directive, not a rebuke.

It's like saying, "You think you're a smart student? Then study so your grades won't drop." The word *study* in that context isn't a scolding; it's an instruction on planting knowledge.

Are we ignoring instructions after the dance?

To ignore instructions is to ignore the instructor. To ignore the message is to ignore the messenger. To ignore a scheduled church service is to disregard an experience that God has ordered for you and those who were meant to experience your love in person, during that service. Ignoring ignorance itself can and will lead to destruction. It's easy to overlook a situation when we don't realize that *situations* can cause us to neglect our responsibility to that situation.

A friend of mine once began acting distant toward me. I didn't know why, so I asked him. He responded, "Shane, have you ever stopped to think that maybe I'm going through something?" I was so focused on feeling like I was the victim that I ignored the possibility that he was carrying his own heavy burden.

Sometimes, when problems face us, recognizing what others are facing becomes difficult. That's when we must look up and inward to the Lord.

1 I will lift up mine eyes unto the hills, from whence cometh my help.
2 My help cometh from the Lord, which made heaven and earth.
Psalm 121:1–2 KJV

Everyone handles their problems differently. When I go through trials, I find joy in ministering to others. It's one of the most powerful ways I've discovered to stir the gifts God has placed in my life. Ministering while burdened fills my spirit with joy. I ride the waves of that anointing and speak whatever God gives me to say. When I see someone blessed and encouraged, that release becomes my encouragement, too.

There have been times when I've felt alone, afraid, or just "off," and I hate that feeling. It's dangerous because it dulls my sensitivity to other people, and being sensitive to others is extremely important to me. When I focus on what I'm going through, I become less aware of what others are facing. So instead of dwelling on negativity, I pour out into others. That's how I maintain my spiritual sensitivity. I don't ever want a situation to close my eyes to someone else's battle.

I genuinely appreciate each of you who is reading this book. I promise to pray for you. Let's agree to pray for one another.

God's Word has always been the truth. Truth doesn't change. If we ignore the Word, we're ignoring the truth—and when we ignore the truth, we ignore God. Are we being ignorant by ignoring knowledge, wisdom, and understanding? Are we ignoring God's Word when we worry about our bills? Here's a hard truth: If we didn't count the cost before we committed to something, we were already ignoring His Word.

> *28 For which of you, intending to build a farm building, does not first sit down and calculate the cost [to see] whether he has sufficient means to finish it?*
>
> *29 Otherwise, when he has laid the foundation and is unable to complete [the building], all who see it will begin to mock and jeer at him,*
>
> *30 Saying, This man began to build and was not able (worth enough) to finish.*
>
> Luke 14:28–30 AMPC

Were you ignorant of your budget? Did you creep—or even sprint—into debt? I thank God for my deliverance. "Debt-free, here I come!"

Let's pause and ponder something together. The Word of God has not merely been said; it is being said. The sermons we've heard are still being preached. There's a specific anointing in the Word of God that never stops flowing. Even after the message is delivered, it remains effective. The Word should still be burning in the hearts of those who heard it. So here's the question: What are you doing after the sermon?

Be careful with your answer because you carry a responsibility. You are accountable to act in alignment with what you heard. The Word gave you the ability. You heard it. You understood it. You now have the ability. The next move is yours. What will be your response to your ability?

The sermon ends, the altar call is made, and it's time to go home. But while I'm at the altar, I think about the changes I need to make when I leave. I reflect on what I will do to please God. For me, the altar isn't just a place where someone gets saved; it's a sacred place of decision, a holy ground where we make permanent choices.

The Word of God doesn't stop working when the sermon ends. It's time for us to stop ignoring what God has spoken into our lives. Let's embrace our responsibilities and allow God's Word to keep transforming us—in us, on us, and through us. In Chapter 1, I mentioned that the fruit of the Spirit reflects our responses to the Spirit. How are you responding to the Word? Are you showing love? Are you walking in peace and self-control? Responding rightly is about taking full responsibility for what you know.

Pastors are shepherds who carry the weight of their members' spiritual growth, and sometimes they get discouraged. There are times I have preached under the power of the Holy Spirit, only to hear a member say a few days later, "No, I don't remember what you preached Sunday morning." Such a statement can dampen a leader's belief that the congregants are receiving and living what they're preaching.

Many members seek counseling, and are you one of those who expect the pastor to do all the praying and all the Scripture quoting? Don't be spiritually L.A.Z.Y. (Losing All Zeal Yieldingly). God called us to mature in our relationship with Him.

If you fall, the Bible says to get up. So get up and try again! If trying feels too hard, reach out for strength from someone who's spiritually stronger. We must all come to a point where we learn about God for ourselves. Never forget that.

Often, we focus so much on our trials, disappointments, and setbacks that we end up ignoring the Word. However, if we shift our attention to God's Word, we would, by comparison, overlook the trials. That doesn't mean pretending they don't exist. It means you consciously choose to fix your focus on God. And when you do that, the weight of your problems often lifts. Maybe this kind of selective focus is what we should call *good ignorance*.

When we focus on God, we begin to see ourselves through *His* eyes. His agenda is the master plan, and His plan includes us. When you give your life to God, He will use it for His purposes. That's how God responds to His ability—by acting on it. And if He has your life, then He also has the responsibility to take care of it.

That's why, years ago, I told God, "You have my life." And since then, when the devil tries to drag a problem into my focus, I don't even blink. I just tell him, "I don't have my life anymore. God has it. Take it up with Him."

The devil does not care about us. He wants us to worry. He'll show up, most times unexpectedly, just to make sure we worry. But if God has our lives, we can be encouraged to know that all is well. Let's tell the enemy that we no longer have our lives, so we can't legally do what they want us to do, due to a transfer of ownership. We're in God's hands, and He takes perfectly great care of us.

Respond with your ability. That's what responsibility is. So many of us get into trouble with the Lord not because we lack knowledge, but because of how we respond to situations. Our default responses are often discouragement, frustration, fear, or anger—none of which are parts of the Holy Spirit's fruit. Earlier in this book, I mentioned that the fruit of the Spirit should be our responses. Christians aren't supposed to react the way the world does. We walk by faith, not by sight.

> *For we walk by faith [we regulate our lives and conduct ourselves by our conviction or belief respecting man's relationship to God and divine things, with trust and holy fervor; thus we walk] not by sight or appearance.*
>
> 2 Corinthians 5:7 AMPC

I admit that I struggle with holding back my frustration. I don't enjoy confronting people. My heart desires to live in a way that reflects only the character of Christ. I work daily to crucify my flesh's desires. I don't want my stubborn nature to override the sweetness of Christ's Spirit within me. I don't want there to be a "bad side" to Shane. I pray that, by His Holy Spirit, the Lord will help me to achieve this daily.

So here's a challenge: Live out this experience tomorrow. Consciously and intentionally, let your response to every person and every situation reveal only the fruit of the Spirit. No matter what comes at you, respond with love, joy, peace, longsuffering, gentleness, goodness, faith, meekness, and temperance. That, right there, is what it means to walk in the Spirit.

Walking in the Spirit doesn't mean speaking in tongues all day or reading the Bible every moment. It's not acting "super spiritual." It means living out God's Word. It means living by faith. And walking by faith is walking in the Spirit, because faith is spiritual.

Has the enemy ever tempted you with something that didn't even appeal to you? That's because the things he used to tempt you with no longer worked. And when that happens, the devil gets frustrated. So what does he do? He either throws everything at you at once or tries something so weak, so unrelated, it's laughable. Why? Because you're walking by faith and walking in the Spirit—and it's working. It's messing with him. Keep the devil nervous. Keep him confused. Keep him running. Shake him off.

> *So be subject to God. Resist the devil [stand firm against him], and he will flee from you.*
>
> James 4:7 AMPC

I recall a day of great victory. I overcame several temptations on that particular day. As I entered a grocery store, a demon tried to tempt me to steal something. I laughed out loud. I hadn't been a thief, nor had that type of temptation ever enticed me. I knew exactly what was happening. The Lord had brought me through so many victories that day, and the devil was confused. That demon had run out of strategies. I've experienced that on more than one occasion. To God—and God alone—be all the glory!

People often say that trials come to make us strong. But Scripture gives us greater clarity. The parable of the sower explains why "stony ground" isn't a good place for the Word of God to grow.

> *Yet it has no real root in him, but is temporary (inconstant, lasts but a little while); and when affliction or trouble or persecution comes on account of the Word, at once he is caused to stumble [he is*

> *repelled and begins to distrust and desert Him Whom he ought to trust and obey] and he falls away.*
>
> Matthew 13:21 AMPC

The Word of God is powerful, and the devil is aware of its potency. Demons know that once the Word is planted in our spirits, it will become a powerful force. When we choose to walk in agreement with it, our actions will be empowered by the Word, and that will defeat the enemy. So he'll do everything he can to take the Word from us. Therefore, trials are designed to intentionally weaken us, not strengthen us.

If a demon succeeds in taking the Word from us, we lose our power because power is in and through God's Word. That's why Matthew 13:21 says trouble comes *on account of the Word*. It's the Word he's after. If you just heard a sermon and decided to quit sinning, the enemy's going to launch a campaign to stop you. He'll stir up affliction, trouble, or persecution—anything to take that Word away.

But when we receive the Word in the good ground of an obedient heart, no situation that challenges the Word will shake us. Good ground is a heart that accepts the Word with a faithful determination to obey it. Demons can't know that God has delivered us until they've tempted us. Demons can't see what's in our minds; only God can (1 Kings 8:39). They know when we've attentively listened to them when we respond to others in obedience to the demons' temptations. If we respond to temptation with obedience to God, we confirm that His Word is rooted in the good ground of our hearts.

If we disobey after being tempted, the Word did not take root, so the enemy steals it. When trials come, will you respond with your ability? Also, are you aware of your abilities?

Those who plant the Word in good ground are those who hear it, understand it, and act on it. We have the ability to obey every time we're tested. Anything short of obedience won't produce sustained fruit. Never let a person, a situation, or even your feelings steal God's Word from your heart/mind, soul, and spirit.

The thief comes only in order to steal and kill and destroy. I came that they may have and enjoy life, and have it in abundance (to the full, till it overflows).

John 10:10 AMPC

Our human spirits are like soil, which God designed to grow whatever we plant in it. Who you are is the result of what you've allowed to be planted in you. If you're producing evil or sinful fruit, it's because you allowed evil and sinful seeds to be planted and grow roots in you. And if your tree bears evil fruit, that's what it will be called.

Don't let the enemy tamper with any part of you. The Bible gives direction for every part of our being:

Let this mind be in you, which was also in Christ Jesus.

Philippians 2:5 KJV

Let's not be ignorant after the dance.

CHAPTER 11:

GLORY AFTER THE DANCE

> 5 *Thus says God the Lord—He Who created the heavens and stretched them forth, He Who spread abroad the earth and that which comes out of it, He Who gives breath to the people on it and spirit to those who walk in it:*
> 6 *I the Lord have called You [the Messiah] for a righteous purpose and in righteousness; I will take You by the hand and will keep You; I will give You for a covenant to the people [Israel], for a light to the nations [Gentiles],*
> 7 *To open the eyes of the blind, to bring out prisoners from the dungeon, and those who sit in darkness from the prison.*
> 8 *I am the Lord; that is My name! And My glory I will not give to another, nor My praise to graven images.*
>
> Isaiah 42:5–8 AMPC

Glory causes a person or a thing to be labeled as an image or an icon when it relates to fame. Have you ever seen a famous individual in person, and your admiration of their talent made you say, "Wow!" because of the glory of who that person is or what they represent? Perhaps the person was just sitting down to eat. Even seeing a celebrity in that posture made you starstruck. That is glory.

Glory, in the Bible, is described as being heavy or weighty. In terms of wealth, having a lot of money makes you weighty. If you're famous, your notoriety gives you weight. One meaning of glory that resonates with me is how a person or thing appears, catching the eye and attracting attention, commanding recognition. It's the kind of appearance that grabs your attention. You might have heard the saying, "You look like a million bucks!" That splendor and brilliance intentionally draw you in and can hold your gaze.

Glory can elevate someone or something to an iconic image, especially when it comes to fame and recognition. Have you ever seen a celebrity and been struck with awe? That's because of their glory—who they are or what they represent. Even seeing a famous person simply walking to their next flight in a crowded airport can cause people's admiration for the individual to escalate immediately. That's glory.

> *Since all have sinned and are falling short of the honor glory which God bestows and received.*
>
> Romans 3:23 AMPC

This scripture speaks of coming short of the glory of God or lacking the glory of God. It describes when we miss the mark, like an archer missing the bullseye. What we lack is God's image and character. When God speaks, He speaks from who He is and how He wants things to be. To obey Him is to reflect Him. To reflect Him is to glorify Him. When we disobey Him, we fall short of giving Him glory. All disobedience to God is sin, and sin can never glorify God.

Your presence represents who you are. When you walk into a room, who you are shows up with you in that moment. Have you ever noticed people nudging each other or whispering when you enter a space? That's your presence speaking—carrying your past, your present, and even a hint of your future. Even the mention of your name represents who you are. That's why the name of Jesus is so powerful. Let's bless (speak well of) the wonderful name, Jesus!

The name Jesus embodies all that He is. And who He is declares what He can do. We can sum up all that Jesus has done, is doing, and will do by mentioning His name. Just saying "Jesus" fills the atmosphere with life. Thinking about the power, love, and hope in His name stirs up praise in me. Hallelujah!

Your name works the same way. When someone sees it written or hears it spoken, everything connected to you, good or bad, comes to mind. That's why we must carefully obey Jesus' words in Matthew 5:16. He said to let your light shine so that people would see your good works and glorify the Father, not you. Let's only shine with works pleasing to God, not the actions we're tempted to take to please ourselves.

God has promised to give you so much. He's even willing to share His kingdom with you. But there's one thing He will never give away: His glory. And yet, His glory is revealed every time He blesses you.

> *And my God will liberally supply (fill to the full) your every need according to His riches in glory in Christ Jesus.*
>
> Philippians 4:19 AMPC

Yes, you danced because God revealed His glory. But did you know that His glory can also be revealed after the dance?

God speaks a word to you; then He watches to see if you'll obey it. When you do, those are your good works. But it doesn't end there. After obedience, you must give Him glory—give Him the esteemed credit for the outcome. If you keep the glory for yourself and claim it was your power or wisdom that made it happen, you're in danger. The glory belongs only to the Lord.

> *17 And beware lest you say in your [mind and] heart, My power and the might of my hand have gotten me this wealth.*
> *18 But you shall [earnestly] remember the Lord your God, for it is He Who gives you power to get wealth, that He may establish His covenant which He swore to your fathers, as it is this day.*
> *19 And if you forget the Lord your God and walk after other gods and serve them and worship them, I testify against you this day that you shall surely perish.*
> *20 Like the nations which the Lord makes to perish before you, so shall you perish, because you would not obey the voice of the Lord your God.*
>
> Deuteronomy 8:17–20 AMPC

Why does God do things the way He does? Does He wait to move so that He'll get the glory? Is that why He doesn't always come when we want Him to? I've never read in Scripture where God healed a headache. Of course, He can—but the point is that God loves to step in when there's no one else who can fix it. He's drawn to impossibilities.

As we give Him glory, He does even more—so we can glorify Him even more. Just be careful not to praise Him merely to get something in return. He deserves glory simply because of Who He is. We were created to glorify Him, and He is worthy of it, for He's the One who gives us breath and life.

> *It is not good to eat much honey; so for men to seek glory, their own glory, causes suffering and is not glory.*
>
> Proverbs 25:27 AMPC

Always give the glory to God. André Crouch wrote a powerful reminder in one of his songs, "Give it all back to Me. What I've done for you, what I'll do through you, give it all back to Me." That's exactly what we're called to do. Give God all the glory for what He's done in, to, and through our lives. He alone is worthy of all glory, honor, and praise!

Now is the time to do all we can for the ministry of Jesus Christ, knowing we are serving God directly. These are our good works, and we must be sure we're doing them to bring glory to Him, not ourselves. He empowers us to do all that He requires us to do, so He deserves the praise. All of those who receive from God should return praiseworthy glory to Him.

Certain rap artists, despite using vulgar language in their music, often begin award speeches by giving glory to God. They thank Him for their talent. Many Christians criticize them, saying their music doesn't glorify God. It doesn't, yet, I believe that they're very aware that their creativity comes from God. Some might argue, "Their gifts came from satan," but who created lucifer in the first place? And who created music? God created both.

The Creator deserves all the glory for the gift, not the profanity. As believers, we should pray that those artists go deeper than recognizing God merely as Creator. Let's pray they come to know Him as Father, as Savior, and as the One Who lovingly redeems. Let's intercede for them to have a healthy relationship with God, not just giving Him eventful recognition.

Some people are hesitant to do things for the church because they fear they won't get credit. If that's you, ask the Holy Spirit to redirect that drive. Let your motive shift to giving God glory. When you serve in ministry with that mindset, you're serving God directly. There will be no need to chase recognition when your heart is settled in His presence.

So then, whether you eat or drink, or whatever you may do, do all for the honor and glory of God.
1 Corinthians 10:31 AMPC

We must reach the place where we can honestly say, from the bottom of our hearts, "As long as God gets the glory, I am well satisfied." When we refuse to obey God's Word, we're withholding the glory He deserves from our obedience. Letting our lights shine—living lives of obedience—brings glory to God. And remember, He will not share His glory with anyone. Don't rob Him of it.

To glorify God, we must do what He asks. That means obedience. Everyone wants a rhema word—a fresh, personal word from God for a specific situation. And that's good. But the rhema must be rooted in the logos—God's written Word. A clear definition of rhema is *the logos revealed at the right time by the Holy Spirit*. If you don't know the logos, you won't correctly understand the rhema. Obey both the logos and the rhema—and you'll give God the glory.

Let me give an example. The written Word (logos) tells us that God desires to heal. That's the established truth. But in John 9:1-11, Jesus performed a healing that required a specific action. He spat on the ground, made mud, and put it on the blind man's eyes. Then came the rhema—the instruction to go and wash. When the man obeyed, healing manifested.

Let's return to the topic of *good works*. Your good works create glory for God. When your light shines through those works, God gets the glory. Consider this: A tube is essential to deliver toothpaste, but without the paste inside, the tube is useless. The squeezing and pressure applied to the tube bring out the product meant to serve others. And once it's empty—once it has completed its job—it's discarded.

How does a tube give glory to what's inside it? The label printed on the outside tells us what's inside. Almost everything on that tube describes what it holds. The only instruction we might find about the tube itself is: "For best results, start at the bottom and go up." (Those instructions reflect how God conditions our lives, whether it's starting at the bottom and working our way up in school, a place of employment, etc.)

You're God's tube. Everything He put in you is meant to be released through you under pressure for His glory. As He elevates you, He wants what's in you to come out and reflect Him.

If I pick up a tube labeled Crest® and something else comes out, I'll assume it's an impostor. It claimed one thing on the outside but delivered something entirely different under pressure. That's false advertising. Now, ask yourself: Do you proclaim to be a Christian? Then what comes out of you when pressure is applied?

> *You yourselves are our letter of recommendation (our credentials), written in your hearts, to be known (perceived, recognized) and read by everybody.*
>
> 2 Corinthians 3:2 AMPC

People don't just see you; they read the life you live. If you're truly walking with the Lord, the joy on your face will preach before you say a word. Your smile will reflect His light. Your countenance will minister to others, and they'll want what you have. Your obedience and faithfulness won't go unnoticed when your life radiates with the glory of God.

I remember a classmate of mine at Brookdale Middle School in my hometown telling me, "There's something about your smile. When I'm having a rough day and I see it, it lifts me." I was stunned. I had no idea my smile was ministering to anyone, especially with my schoolmate being that young, yet bold, mature, and expressive enough to share. We never know who we're affecting and how. Again, let's strive to do all God wants us to do to give HIm glory.

Two more incidents happened during my respiratory therapy clinicals. In one case, I sat quietly in the physical therapy department, waiting for an assignment. A therapist passed by, and I greeted him with a simple "Good morning." He replied, but then returned a moment later, visibly puzzled. He asked, "Are you saved?" I smiled and said, "Yes, I am. How did you know?" He seemed relieved and explained, "When I looked at you, I couldn't see your face because it was glowing with light. I've never seen anything like it." I was speechless. He continued, "I figured you had to be saved or something. That glow said it all."

The second incident happened not long after. A nurse jokingly insulted me in front of others. Another nurse I'd never met overheard and said, "You'd better leave him alone. He's a preacher." Shocked, I asked her how she knew. I assumed a classmate had told her. She quickly corrected me: "Nobody told me. I can just tell. My father and brothers are preachers. I've been around them all my life. You even talk like one."

What would you think if everything written on a tube of toothpaste only spoke about the tube itself, without ever mentioning what's inside? You wouldn't value that tube. Why? Because it says nothing about what it holds. In the same way, some people talk only about themselves—what they can do, what they've accomplished—and they give no honor to the One who gave them the gift. That's not glorifying God. The Word warns us clearly:

Pride goes before destruction, and a haughty spirit before a fall.

Proverbs 16:18 AMPC

The tube serves a beneficial and valuable purpose: to hold and deliver its contents. I doubt anyone will carry a handful of toothpaste in their pocket.

If a label didn't reveal the contents, we would overlook it and never purchase the tube. The tube that displays and contains its contents is used to the extent of its value. The value of the tube expires once its benefits to us expire. Then, we discard the empty tube. When we understand that our worth is in what God has placed within us—not in who we are socially—we live with a purpose that glorifies our Father in Heaven.

Some people will take the cap off to see what's really in the tube. They might sniff it, squeeze it, and examine its texture. Likewise, when someone is around you long enough, pressure reveals what's inside. If all you ever do is talk about yourself and boast about your worth, you may attract attention, but it won't last. Most people associate with you to see what's in you. Once you reveal the contents of your life, and if it doesn't reflect Christ, certain ones will no longer desire to be in your company. Let this be a mirror for us all. Live only to give God all of the glory!

If you feel like you're "climbing up the rough side of the mountain," remember that everything God puts in you is meant to come out of you for His service, just like the tube. Is it harder to climb the rough side of the mountain than the smooth side? Should we even be climbing mountains at all? A well-known gospel song's lyrics proclaim, "Lord, don't move my mountain, but give me the strength to climb." And while I honor the message of endurance in those lyrics, we also need to recall Jesus' own words:

> *And Jesus answered them, Truly I say to you, if you have faith (a firm relying trust) and do not doubt, you will not only do what has been done to the fig tree, but even if you say to this mountain, Be taken up and cast into the sea, it will be done.*
>
> Matthew 21:21 AMPC

I understand the beauty and context of Negro spirituals—they were born from deep struggle and deeper faith—but sometimes those lyrics reflect "mountain climbing" faith, not "mountain moving" faith. There are seasons when we'd rather carry the weight than believe God will lift it. We've asked repeatedly, and nothing changed—so we stop expecting. But Matthew 21 should stretch our faith.

A preacher once cried out in pain from a stomach virus. While he moaned and begged God to take him home to heaven, his young son was praying for him. Finally, the son snapped and said, "The same breath you're using to ask God to come get you is the same breath you could be using to ask Him to heal you!" That moment struck me deeply.

Start at the bottom and work your way up. That's the only instruction toothpaste tubes usually offer—and it's profound. Starting is often the most challenging part of anything. When I wrote the original version of the book 25 years ago, starting was difficult for me. Not just starting Chapter 1, but beginning any chapter, some days, felt like a battle. I'd sit there with ideas and no drive. On other days, I had the drive but no ideas. I wrestled. It was procrastination—one of the enemy's greatest weapons.

But even once you start, the fight isn't over. Distractions emerge. Discouragement follows. You could list a dozen more enemies right now. But here's the truth: If you've stopped, you can start again. You will begin again—in the name of Jesus! I pray in the name of Jesus that every demon of procrastination, hindrance, and fear will be canceled from operating in your life right now—in Jesus' name!

"A just man falls but a few times, but he gets back up with the right mind." That line comes from a song by the gospel group Commissioned. This verse inspired the lyrics:

> *For a righteous man falls seven times and rises again, but the wicked are overthrown by calamity.*
>
> Proverbs 24:16 AMPC

God receives glory when you rise after a fall. Just because you danced doesn't mean you won't need His glory again. You, the reader, may already know this, but let me remind you: Getting up displays God's glory through the strength He placed within you.

There is glory after the dance for more than one reason. One of those reasons is this: You might fall. I've heard many preachers say, "Just because you're knocked down doesn't mean you're knocked out." If that's you—if you've been knocked down—then use your spiritual strength. That strength is called joy, and as I mentioned before, joy is not a fleeting emotion. Joy is spiritual. You can experience joy even when life is hard. It's like when a saint passes away. Naturally, their loved ones grieve. Yet, there's still joy because we know that loved one is "resting in the bosom of the Lord." That joy comes from knowing the truth of God's promises.

So if you've been knocked down, be encouraged. It is glorious when you get back up. Why? Because getting up means you're choosing to keep going. You're choosing God's plan all over again. That decision reveals the glory of God in your life, and that always frightens the enemy.

Why does the devil panic when you get up? Getting up proves you resisted him. You resisted his agenda. You refused to stay where he thought he had you.

> *So be subject to God. Resist the devil [stand firm against him], and he will flee from you.*
>
> James 4:7 AMPC

Are you feeling like you can't rise from where you've fallen? Then I believe the next chapter will encourage you. God still wants to reveal His glory to you and through you…after the dance.

CHAPTER 12:

THE BEAUTY OF AN OPENED GRAVE

12 Therefore prophesy and say to them, Thus says the Lord God: Behold, I will open your graves and cause you to come up out of your graves, O My people; and I will bring you [back home] to the land of Israel.
13 And you shall know that I am the Lord [your Sovereign Ruler], when I have opened your graves and caused you to come up out of your graves, O My people.
14 And I shall put My Spirit in you and you shall live, and I shall place you in your own land. Then you shall know, understand, and realize that I the Lord have spoken it and performed it, says the Lord.

Ezekiel 37:12–14 AMPC

A grave is defined as a hole in the ground where the dead are buried. Even if nothing has yet been placed in it, it's still considered a grave. But that's not the focus here. In this message, an opened grave refers to one that has already received something dead—something that was once alive—and has since been uncovered.

Let's take a closer look at the word *dead*. It means to have neither life nor any positive activity resulting from life. For some of you reading this, your influence is dead. Your gift is dead. Your patience is dead. Your drive is dead. Your kindness is dead. Your inspiration is dead. Your walk in the Spirit is dead. Your prayer life is dead. Your generosity is dead. Your consecration is dead. Your sincerity is dead. Your ministry is dead. Your relationship with God is dead. (In terms of this chapter's message, something can only be declared dead if it was once alive.)

Someone once said, "Anything dead needs to be buried." Let's examine that burial. A hole is dug. The dead are placed in it. Then it's covered. But what is it covered with? Dirt. Junk. Trash.

You asked. You received. And so, you danced. You danced because of the joy of receiving from the Lord. But somewhere along the way, what you received from God died. It lost life, grew inactive, and became unresponsive. This happens to everyone at one point or another. A part of you that once burned bright goes cold.

Then someone comes along to offer their unsolicited burial services. How? Through gossip. "I've got some dirt on that person," they say. "You want to hear it?" Another joins in: "I've got junk and trash on them too." Dirt, junk, and trash are slang words for the harmful, shameful, and reckless actions people want to hide or forget. And whether the gossip is true or not, engaging in it is still a sin.

> *He who goes about as a talebearer reveals secrets, but he who is trustworthy and faithful in spirit keeps the matter hidden.*
>
> Proverbs 11:13 AMPC

This verse makes it clear that even accurate information is not always to be shared. A faithful person covers, rather than exposes.

> *Let no foul or polluting language, nor evil word nor unwholesome or worthless talk [ever] come out of your mouth, but only such [speech] as is good and beneficial to the spiritual progress of others, as is fitting to the need and the occasion, that it may be a blessing and give grace (God's favor) to those who hear it.*
>
> Ephesians 4:29 AMPC

Gossip never builds up—it pollutes. This verse warns us to speak only what strengthens and blesses.

He who covers and forgives an offense seeks love, but he who repeats or harps on a matter separates even close friends.

Proverbs 17:9 AMPC

Even repeating what someone did wrong—true or not—brings division and is discouraged. Covering someone's failure shows love and maturity.

Maybe you're in a place where things are dead in your life, and you became bound by sin, and you know it. You hate it, and you desperately want deliverance from it. The last thing you need is someone reminding you of your fall, let alone burying you in it. When people come and cover you with their gossip, their slander, and their assumptions, they're not helping. They're digging your grave and piling on the dirt.

I've watched young women who became pregnant before marriage walk through deep shame, not because of their pregnancy, but because of the gossip. They felt isolated, helpless, abandoned, and even betrayed by close friends who shared their story. I've tried to encourage these young ladies. And let me tell you, it's not easy. I've seen their countenance drained by judgment, not just from outsiders but from people they once called best friends.

"Who's going to pray me out of the grave I'm in?" That question isn't meant to be answered with words. It should be answered with action.

It's heartbreaking to see a single mother grow resentful of her child, not because of the baby, but because of the pain and shame inflicted by others. The child was never the sinful act. The sin was the act of sex outside of marriage. And even then, our response should never be to shame, but to restore (Galatians 6:1). We have to remind these women that God still loves them and that their child is a gift, not a punishment. That baby may be a future minister of the gospel.

In Ezekiel 37:12, God promised that He would open your graves and cause you to come up out of them. In verse 14, He promised to put His Spirit in you. He also said that you would live. Then, He promised to place you in your own land. Good news: You are coming up out of your grave! God Himself is going to bring you up!

What is the beauty of an opened grave? The beauty of an opened grave is revealed when the "burial volunteers" arrive—those people who came to dig up your past and throw more dirt on you. They're ready to gossip, judge, and accuse. But when they show up, all they find is an empty hole. The dirt, junk, and trash are still there—but you're not! The person who was once there is no longer buried. What was dead is now alive, active, obedient, and resurrected from the grave. All they can see now is the beauty of an opened grave.

Your past is not your future. Don't let your past dictate your destiny. Don't let it trap you in shame. If you've asked God for forgiveness, then according to His Word:

Therefore, [there is] now no condemnation (no adjudging guilty of wrong) for those who are in Christ Jesus, who live [and] walk not after the dictates of the flesh, but after the dictates of the Spirit.

Romans 8:1 AMPC

Focus on what God is going to do in your future. If you're in a buried situation, believe God to free you from your grave. And if you're not, pray for someone who already has volunteers trying to bury them.

Whatever has died in your life is subject to resurrection the moment God speaks His Word into it. His Word carries resurrection power. When He speaks, the grave has no choice but to let you go. And if all it takes is a word from God to raise you, then you have great faith—faith that God always responds to.

Then to the centurion Jesus said, Go; it shall be done for you as you have believed. And the servant boy was restored to health at that very moment.

Matthew 8:13 AMPC

Now, if someone tries to throw more dirt on you, since you're alive, just shake it off! The devil will try to discourage you. He'll bring up your past, your failures, and your burial—but let that grave remind you of the resurrection power of your God. That's all you see now—the beauty of not being in that grave.

I've overcome some strong vices. And yes, those demons still try to tempt me. But I know I've been delivered. I've received freedom, and I'm staying free! The vice may still be at the gravesite, but I'm not. I'm here. I'm where God placed me, doing His will. "Here" is wherever the vice is not. Here I am—free! And I'll remain free as long as I follow the voice of the Lord.

You cannot grow in a grave. Even if you could, what would it matter? Can you minister from the grave? Can you shine your light while buried under shame? Jesus has the power over death, hell, and the grave. Let Him bring you out!

And He's not just bringing you out for no reason. He promised to put His Spirit in you. That means you'll be alive and empowered! It's time to obey and serve the Lord. That's why we're alive—to be used for His good pleasure.

What about prosperity? Yes, God wants us to prosper in due time. Prosperity pleases Him.

Let those who favor my righteous cause and have pleasure in my uprightness shout for joy and be glad and say continually, Let the Lord be magnified, Who takes pleasure in the prosperity of His servant.

Psalm 35:27 AMPC

But don't chase prosperity; chase the God of prosperity. Your day of wealth will come, but it will come in God's timing. And His timing is always best.

Now let's be honest. Most dead things have been buried. But here's the truth: Some things were buried alive. One of the worst kinds of burial is called paranoia. That's when you live in fear without any sound reason. You start to dread hearing someone's name. You expect rejection. You shrink when your ideas are mentioned. You avoid sharing your dreams because you're sure they'll be laughed at. That's not life. That's being buried alive—buried under fear while you're still breathing.

I once worked at a fast food restaurant as a management trainee. One of our regional supervisors was a walking terror. Just the mention of his name sent people running. If we heard he was coming, even off-duty employees would flee the restaurant. When he walked in, the temptation to fear him accompanied him. Even if he asked a question I knew the answer to, I'd freeze. His presence would paralyze what I had already learned, and I hated it. I expected to be embarrassed, belittled, or punished, but strangely enough, it never happened.

What should be done about paranoia? Even when you do good deeds from a pure heart, it can seem like certain people are never pleased. If you're not careful, you'll begin to seek their approval more than God's. That's dangerous. You must know God for yourself. If you're buried in a deep, dark grave of fear, you can be delivered. You must be freed. No one can live freely under such a weight.

Paranoia didn't want me to write this book. I couldn't afford to fear what people might say. My focus had to be—and still is—God's plan for my life. When God told me to write this book, paranoia tried everything it could to stop me. The devil pressured me to abandon the idea altogether. I had to defeat paranoia daily. It didn't strike once or twice; it came repeatedly. But each time, I had a decision to make. And I decided to obey the Lord.

Overcoming paranoia wasn't easy for me. It might not be easy for you either, but it must be done. And God will help you do it. If you don't conquer it, you may not obey the voice of the Lord when He says, "Go and do." Don't be afraid of what people might say—even if they claim your obedience is not from God. Just make sure you've heard the Lord clearly and confirmed His voice through prayer. When you've done that, move forward without fear. God will protect you and prosper you when you obey His voice. He promised—and He cannot lie. Who else will God use if we don't let Him use us?

When we please God, those who are worthy of being pleased will also be pleased. Remember that.

If you feel trapped inside of yourself, but you know God has told you to "Go and do," pray to confirm His voice. Then do what He said. God will hold you accountable if you ignore His command. He gave it to you, not someone else.

How many times have you said, "I would've done it, but I was afraid"? How many people have you walked past without sharing the gospel with them about Christ? How many lives have you skipped ministering to for the Kingdom of God? How much work is left undone on this earth while you wrestle with fear? Will paranoia bury you forever? Will it keep you from fulfilling God's purpose for your life? I pray not! The scripture that often grips those who do good and yet are criticized is:

Let not then your good be evil spoken of:

Romans 14:16 KJV

This verse is often misunderstood. In the original Greek, the word *let* means *to deny*. In other words, deny that your good is evil. If what you've done is good and in obedience to God, don't allow anyone to label it otherwise. Refuse to agree with false judgment. Don't let the devil, or anyone he uses, distort your obedience.

Please don't let people staple your dreams and visions shut. Be sensitive to the Spirit of God. Sensitivity is developed through prayer. Ask the Holy Spirit to make you more sensitive to His voice—and He will. Sensitivity and humility are two primary keys to living a victorious life in God.

Whoever exalts himself [with haughtiness and empty pride] shall be humbled (brought low), and whoever humbles himself [whoever has a modest opinion of himself and behaves accordingly] shall be raised to honor.

Matthew 23:12 AMPC

No matter what people say to you or about you, the Word of God will never fail. Live according to the Word. If you humble yourself, God will exalt you in front of those who made you feel inferior and everyone else. He will fix your life in such a way that your help will be needed and appreciated. But always remember: He alone is to receive the glory! When you choose to trust Him completely, God will ensure that His glory is present in your life. Just be sure to give it all back to Him. As the scripture says, if we exalt ourselves, God will bring us low. If we humble ourselves, God will exalt us (Matthew 23:12).

God is on your side! He's bringing you up out of your grave and into your own land. Paranoia can only influence you if you remain in its environment. Stay planted in the land God has assigned to you. Serve Him like there is no tomorrow. Fear can destroy what God planned for you if you allow it. But I pray right now in the name of Jesus—no more fear, no more worry, no more paranoia!

Whatever dirt, junk, or trash people may hold against you, God's love can reach beneath it all. Remember, God looks beyond the fault and sees the need. And He sees the need so that He can meet the need. But when you try to meet your own needs apart from Him, all you end up with are more faults. You can come out of the grave you're in. God wants to bring you out! Surrender your entire life to Him—and watch Him work for you.

Before your deliverance, people may have only seen the dirt, junk, and trash. But after your deliverance, they will see you cleansed and standing firm. The dirt, junk, and trash may still be stuck in some people's memories, but as long as it's no longer stuck on you, rejoice! If others want to keep dirty, junky, and trashy minds, that's their choice. You, however, keep your deliverance—and grow!

Are you ready for a grave-bursting experience? Give God that grave situation. Soon you'll be walking in the land He's promised. Don't stay buried after the dance. Even if you find yourself back in a grave-like situation, you can come out victorious.

Trust God's resurrection power…after the dance!

ALTAR CALL AND PRAYER FOR SALVATION

Our Lord Jesus said,

All whom My Father gives (entrusts) to Me will come to Me; and the one who comes to Me I will most certainly not cast out [I will never, no never, reject one of them who comes to Me].

John 6:37 AMPC

Dear Father, I know you will save the one who prays the following prayer according to Your most holy, just, and righteous will for this precious life. I ask, pray, and thank You in the name of my Lord and Savior, Jesus Christ!

If you are a sinner or you want to renew your relationship with God, please pray the following prayer and receive Jesus Christ into your life this very moment. He's waiting for you. He's the only way to Heaven and looks forward to being the primary part of your life here on Earth.

Father God, I come before You now in the name of Jesus Christ. I confess that I am a sinner. Please forgive me and save me from all of my unrepentant sins. I know Jesus Christ is Your Son, Who died for my sins, and that You raised Him from the dead. Lord, Jesus, I invite You into my heart and life right now. Come in and live life through me so that I can please our Father just as You please our Father. I now believe that You have come into my heart and life. Father, I have asked and prayed for these things in the name of Jesus Christ. Thank You, Father, for forgiving me for all of my sins, for saving me, and for freeing me from the power of every demon. Father, I have given my life to You. I no longer have it. Use me, and I will live for You forever! In the name of Jesus Christ, I pray. Amen! I AM SAVED

ABOUT THE AUTHOR

Shane Wall has been preaching internationally for over 40 years and is the author of two bestselling books: the #8 bestseller *Understanding: All Success is Attained by It* (hailed as the first Christian book ever written on the subject of understanding) and the #1 bestseller *The Supernatural Guide to Understanding Angels*. He also recorded a Gospel CD titled *Conversations with God*, featuring songs he personally wrote to express divine conversations between God and His children.

He is the founder and Senior Pastor of **The Feast of the Lord** in Orangeburg, South Carolina, where he resides with his two children, Joshua and Amayah. Apostle Wall regularly ministers in churches and conferences across the globe, helping people break free from spiritual bondage and walk in divine clarity. His free mobile platform, the **Shane Wall App**, offers powerful teachings, insight, and resources for those seeking to grow in their walk with God.

Contact

Shane Wall
PO Box 2005
Orangeburg, SC 29116

・・・

SHANEWALL app

www.shanewall.com

www.ingramcontent.com/pod-product-compliance
Lightning Source LLC
Chambersburg PA
CBHW040246010526
44119CB00057B/830